Poking Holes in the Darkness

Poking Holes in the Darkness

by Collene Martin

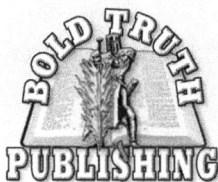

BOLD TRUTH
PUBLISHING

Christian Literature & Artwork
A BOLD TRUTH Publication

Poking Holes in the Darkness
Copyright © 2017 by Collene Martin
ISBN 13: 978-0-9998051-0-7

BOLD TRUTH PUBLISHING
(Christian Literature & Artwork)
606 West 41st, Ste. 4
Sand Springs, Oklahoma 74063
www.BoldTruthPublishing.com

Available from Amazon.com and other retail outlets. Orders by U.S. trade bookstores and wholesalers. Email *boldtruthbooks@yahoo.com*

Quantity sales special discounts are available on quantity purchases by corporations, associations, and others. For details, contact the publisher at the address above.

Cover Art & Design by Aaron Jones.

Printed in the USA.
01 18   10 9 8 7 6 5 4 3 2 1

Table of Contents

Table of Contents

Dedication

Giving honor to God,
I dedicate this book to my husband, Kent Martin
and to the two precious people who raised me
and taught me about Jesus Christ,
Rupert Coke Wright and Ossie Sieber Wright.
I am so grateful for my praying mama
and my heritage from her.
Also to my two brothers,
Rupert C. Wright, Jr., and Connie Milton Wright.
They've all gone on to be with the Lord, as well.
And my beloved, Sister Fuller,
Who was always there to pray for me and my family.

1

Blessings Override Obstacles

"We wrestle not against flesh and blood, but against principalities, against powers..." - Ephesians 6:12a

I have a love for the outdoors and being able to have healthy trees and plentiful fruit. I feel like I have the blessings of God upon me and, along with it, an array of armour to fight against the evil that could entrap my family, my church, my country and those I love.

I have the right to feel especially blessed, for I have 6 beautiful great granddaughters; they are part of my heritage. How magnificent. They are fruit from me and my children. They are of those little people I pray for God to protect.

I wrestled with a Hawthorne bush, which was rough to deal with. That bush had taken up residence around, in and out, up and down a most beautiful apple tree in my yard. It was pruning time, as many of us have felt the urge to have spring cleaning on our yards and in our houses after all the cold weather.

I had worked on the other fruit trees and felt satisfied I

1

could tackle the apple tree. As I got into the pruning process, I could see the Hawthorne bush had the apple tree totally bound. I began to cut and apply myself to the task, I used that apple tree, that needed to be set free to bloom and yield fruit, as a focal point of prayer.

My prayers turned to the Church and the many people who attend and need healing or deliverance from things that have bound them up throughout the years. I also prayed for my family and whatever might hold them from growing in the Lord, being choked by brambles and briars, so to speak.

The pruning process is so the tree can yield bigger and more luscious fruit. I know you know this, but forgive me, I'm from Texas, and I have to learn. The branches should be thinned out to let the tree grow fuller, with more light getting to the center of the plant. Then God's plan for that beautiful apple tree to flourish and produce will not be hampered.

The closer I got to the fruit tree itself, I could see how strong the grip of the Hawthorne bush was. The trunk of the bush was some two to three inches across, so obviously, the bush had grown along with the apple tree from the very beginning.

The individual person is the same. Things attack just like insects and undergrowth, trying to overtake and stunt the spiritual growth of the person planted in the fertile soil of the good graces of the Lord.

For a woman, it might be a sexual attack (I heard only today from the experts that it is one out of seven) or even an actual rape or a case of seeing and experiencing something otherwise traumatic in her younger years. Traumatic things happen to young men, as well. We hear this more and more daily about young men and boys.

We have many young and older military men who have been traumatized by war and the scenes that unfold repeatedly in their minds or sicknesses that have evolved from exposure to different chemicals or explosive devices of conflict. There are things that are reported daily on the news that cause hearts to fail with fear.

God is much greater and takes care of us to the fullest extent. Our trust factor has been affected by fear, doubt and unbelief. There are voices that would tell us we cannot survive the future. There are thoughts that are introduced into our minds that say there is no God, but there is and—He loves us dearly.

I think it is seedy to be so weedy about the foundation upon which this country stands. This great USA is going to stand because we stand for something.

We are vulnerable without Christ in our lives and this is the reason *God sent His only begotten Son* in *John 3:16.* The depth of God's love is seen in the death of His Son as the sacrificial Lamb to justify us before Him.

God provided us with powerful protection to pull down the "strongholds" that have become deeply rooted around us to cause our faith to be weakened, to stunt our growth. When God's fresh wind of revival blows our way so we can really breathe, our faith cannot be snuffed out.

That Hawthorne bush stirred me up, as you can see, and all those things that I have been praying about came to the surface as I worked to free that apple tree. We are the apple of God's eye and He wants us to be free from all entanglements.

I am grateful for all of God's blessings and the opportunity to be His child. *"Goodness and mercy"* shall follow us (track us down; hound us) all the days of our lives *(Ps 23)*. God is in charge and He has commanded His angels to look out for us and share His heavenliness here. He is the High Authority of the Universe. He edifies us into overcomers throughout the obstacles in our little universe. God is on His throne and we're going and growing to reach that height!

2

Don't Scatter the Flock

Just like a flock of sheep, there is safety in numbers. When the Bible said in *Isaiah 53:6, "all we like sheep have gone astray, we have turned every one to his own way, and the*

Lord hath laid on him the iniquity of us all", it was talking about people.

We are like little old sheep that stray here and there and get a little too far from the flock and don't remember how to get back. We have a tendency to look at mankind and his ways and don't keep our eyes on the Lord.

When I lived in Texas, I went to a church that had at least two different splits before I was born. The first produced a Second Baptist and the second one produced a Northside Baptist in a little old town that had only two stoplights.

In *Ezekiel 34:5-6*, the Lord is speaking and says, *"And they were scattered, because there was no shepherd: and they became meat to all the beasts of the field, when they were scattered. My sheep wandered through all the mountains, and upon every high hill: yea, my flock was scattered upon all the face of the earth, and none did search or seek after them".*

We are the sheep of His pasture (the Churchfold) and when we scatter and get out there among the wild critters, sometimes it is hard to return to safety; the fold. What if you were someone who had a hard time with your circumstance. Maybe you had a child who had gotten into trouble and you didn't want to be questioned about it or someone who had a personal condition in which you didn't want inquiry, but just love being in the circle of fellowship. The beauty of the Christian community is also its blemish. Because we are so close due to our commonality, we know much about each other. However, that very fact is supposed to cause us to help together or hurt together.

One Sunday night, Governor Huckabee had a man on his program who had murdered a woman when he was a young man and had found the Lord in prison. This man found forgiveness and salvation and is now a minister of the Gospel in Madison, Tennessee, at Cornerstone Church. He is preaching to over 2000 people every Sunday morning. He is gathering the flock now. He is leading them to the fountain that flows from the throne of God. He was brought into the "commonwealth of faith" for just such a time as this, to bring others in.

Again and again, God spoke of gathering us with great mercies. *Isaiah 54:7* states, *"For a small moment have I forsaken thee; but with great mercies will I gather thee."* It continues in *verse 8* saying, *"In a little wrath I hid My face from thee for a moment; but with everlasting kindness will I have mercy on thee, saith the Lord thy Redeemer."*

Isaiah 54:10 continues with, *"For the mountains shall depart, and the hills be removed; but my kindness shall not depart from thee, neither shall the covenant of my peace be removed, saith the Lord that hath mercy on thee."* His love is that enduring and inviting. He wants us to listen to His statutes and live accordingly. He wants us to realize that He put these in place for our safekeeping.

Jesus loved Jerusalem and mourned the rebellion within her. In *Matthew 23:37* and again in *Luke 13:34,* Jesus said, *"O Jerusalem Jerusalem, thou that killest the prophets, and stonest them which are sent unto thee, how often would I have gathered thy children together even as a hen gathereth her chickens under her wings, and ye would not!"*

As we look around us, we see prophecies being fulfilled; signs of the times are everywhere. There are songs that relay this message, like Midnight Cry. We must draw closer to the Lord and His Church, which Christ gave His life for. We must search out the Gospel truth which brings joy to the soul.

He doesn't want us to suffer through this time. He wants us to be encouraged that He is right here with us. There are people out there that may not understand God still loves them even though they are wounded and floundering. Some of them may have plenty of money and world situations aren't affecting them, but I don't know who they are. It seems to me that everyone, rich and poor, are being affected by finances, healthcare, and many other worries of our world. Look to the Lord and let Him gather you up in His arms and show you His love.

His Son's death was to give you salvation, peace of mind, hope to make it through this life and on into eternal life with Him. There has only been one Savior and one way to Heaven. Christ is the "Door"; the "Way"; the "Truth"; and the "Life"—He is our answer to this warped, topsy-turvy, stressed out, panic-stricken world, which has no real answers to life's deepest questions.

Reach out to others and bring them into the circle of safety. Time is short and many are starving to death for any ray of hope. Jesus is that ray, yea, the Radiance. Help them find Him; gather them with "great mercies."

Don't give up on the CHURCH. Christ never gives up on you! And, if you haven't been to church for a while, churn up a little mister and find out all over again that it really is, like the old-timers say, an "ark of safety." Judgment begins at the House of God and Jesus said for us not to forsake the assembling together. When a church is functioning in the love of God, it is a "shelter in the time of storm." Be a gathered-up sheep into the arms of the "Good Shepherd."

3

Faith, Hope and Love

As we walk through this life, what do we define as the blessings of God? Right now, in the lives of many, they would possibly say they can't see one blessing in their lives. But when you look at it, the Lord woke us up this morning. He's given us another day.

This is a time when hope is being stifled and suffocated. Not enough hope and change! But in spite of all the word-wrangling going on within our earshot, there is hope in Jesus Christ with profound change.

Heartache is everywhere and it comes in many forms. Just as heartache comes when we least expect it, so do blessings. Things just don't look promising to a lot of people right now. There are many things that whisper hopelessness or even scream desperation at us.

Without the Lord, there is no hope. You are on the ropes and about to be counted out. If you look back through the Bible you will find places where God replaced "the enemy about to attack on all sides" with a ray of hope, originally for the Israelites, now for us.

There was the woman who fed Elijah her last cake and she and her son were going to die. When she prepared food for the prophet, her provisions were multiplied. God literally takes a little and makes a lot out of it. He honors obedience like Elijah's. God took five loaves and two fishes and fed five thousand with twelve basketfuls left over.

There was the man whose child was dying and he went to Jesus. He told Jesus, *"If you just say the word, my child will be healed."* It happened because of the man's faith in the Lord. So, the situation is by no means as dire as it appears to be when God is included as a factor.

Then there is Moses at the Red Sea and Pharoah's men were pressing down on them to keep them in slavery. Moses touched the sea with his staff and the waters opened; then after they got across safely, the enemy was drowned.

There may be those of you who have prayed and prayed and your situation is not changing and it seems just as hopeless as it was when you began. God can still give you hope if you will wait for the answer with the virtue of patience. He always pays attention to the petitioner and will make sure the results will be the solution, the best solution. It may not turn out like you think it should, but the Lord will walk you through it to the other side of a catastrophe.

Faith, hope, charity, blessings . . . these are not just platitudes of a positive attitude, as some would say. These are actual powerful words that originate from the endless storehouse of God.

If you have followed my articles through the years, you ask yourself, *"How can she be so up tempo about everything? I can tell from her candid divulgences through the years that she has had similar experiences to mine and it hasn't quite been heavenly around here. Is she really out of her mind?"*

Well, I have dipped into the well where living waters flow and my thirsting for righteousness is always filled. Come, jump in with me! Let's get into the waters, past the ankles, like waist deep. Our Most High God is satisfying. I have seen Him move in my behalf.

God loves mankind and wants to bless us. He first wants us to love Him and serve Him. Then the channel is open for the constant-flowing reaping of rewards. Yes, here on Earth. We don't have to wait for Heaven.

There are those who realize that Christ is real and that the love that was shown forth on Calvary is not just an experience, but a real and present existence.

For many, it is hard to believe that this God Who lives way up there would give something so precious to Himself for us, to make a way for us to be with Him in glory. But He did. For others who were told from childhood on up, it is a way of life, a way to survive the rough times.

God is not way out there. He is right here with us. He has made Himself available to answer our prayers and to be a part of our lives.

Why would God care? He created us from the very earth that He created, to fellowship with Him. He sought us out and drew us to Him by His precious Holy Spirit.

He can clean our hearts up; He forgives, He loves. He brings us to a place of standing in our lives rather than lying in the dirt of our sin. He doesn't want us to walk through life with our heads hung down; He doesn't want us to be defeated.

God wants us to be overcomers—a healed and whole people.

I had a friend who walked through the small town where I lived and she always looked at the ground and because of things she had been through in her life, she didn't feel worthy of anything but to drink. That was how she dealt with her past as a child and through the years. My heart went out to her. Her favorite song was *"Amazing Grace."*

God can take the scars on your heart and heal them—if you will let Him. He can mend your memories that are so full of pain and make you brand new! You just have to acknowledge Him and ask Him to do it. He loves you, just as you love your children and family and would do anything for them. He loves each of you individually that much.

He is Faith, Hope, and Love all bunched into one precious Savior and God. Because of God's love, we can make it through each day. Little things, the smallest things may bring us hope. Unlikely things bring the answers to prayer.

1 Corinthians 13:13 says, *"And now abideth faith, hope, love, these three: but the greatest of these is love".*

God gave His Only Begotten Son, because He loved us before we ever walked this earth. Jesus lived, bled and died to bring us His Hope. God gave us the most important element to faith and that is the one to have faith in, Jesus Christ.

4

Get Dressed for the Battle

When you get ready to go to work or just face the day, you have to get dressed. You have to pick out the right clothes and be prepared to look presentable or acceptable. Am I right? Of course, you may be thinking what color dress and shoes as a woman or what color shirt, tie or suit as a man. I am really talking about far more than that. I am talking about getting properly attired on any given day as a fortified, presentable child of God. You need an invisible outer layer. Just because it is unseen doesn't mean it is not effective. I am referring to the "whole armor of God."

Each piece of the armor has a purpose. *Ephesians 6* names each part. *"Wherefore take unto you the whole armour of God, that you may be able to withstand in the evil day, and having done all, to stand. Stand therefore girt about with truth, and having on the breastplate of righteousness; And your feet shod with the preparation of the gospel of peace; Above all, taking the shield of faith, wherewith ye shall be able to quench all the firey darts of the wicked [evil one]. And take the helmet of salvation, and the sword of the Spirit, which is the word of God: Praying always with all prayer and supplication in the Spirit, and watching thereunto with all perseverance and supplication for all saints." (vs 13-18)*

First, we **take unto us the whole armour of God**, not just pieces or patches, to be effective.

We must be **girt about with truth**, holding our spiritual clothes and ourselves together with no lies or deceit.

Then **have on the breastplate of righteousness** which means we have accepted Christ into our life as Savior (that we are in right standing with God through the blood of Jesus Christ).

Next, we are to be **shod with the preparation of the Gospel of peace**, not walking in anger and revenge. Not speaking evil of others or talking with filthy words. Only Jesus can provide that kind of peace that passes all understanding and can keep our speech clean.

[Then] we **take the shield of faith**: with the shield of faith, we can withstand the barrage of overwhelming attacks that are directed at our very souls by the prince of the power of the air.

We must **take the helmet of salvation** to protect our minds from the many thoughts that would turn us aside to walk a path that is unbecoming of a Christian. Often, our mind is the first point of assault and we begin to dwell on a thought and then it becomes a trailblazer in the wrong direction.

We carry **the sword of the Spirit** in our hearts, minds and hands, speaking and handling the Word of God to defeat our enemies (the evil influences), that could overtake us.

All of this is because, *"We wrestle not against flesh and blood, but against principalities, against powers, against the rulers [leaders] of the darkness of this world, against spiritual [whole army of] wickedness in high [commanding] places." - Ephesians 6:12*

We come from "all walks of life," we are all walking, we never know what we might run into. We are walking into unknown territory every day—we must be prepared for anything. We never know what a phone call will bring. We must be fully clothed with our spiritual apparel to deal with the daily frenzy, fitfulness and frightfulness.

Our interpersonal relationships can be a cause of consternation. They create much pressure in our daily lives. It is hard to say "no" to anything, if you are like me, but you can't say "yes" to everything. We need to be girt about with truth (have our belt on) and shod or shoed with the preparation of peace to deal with them. We must be fully dressed in our armour to deal with people.

I was a Walmarter and dressed up in my full armour every day along with my Walmart duds for work. You know, I believe, there are some of my customers who came through my line who saw my outer layer of "might for the right". These were the ones with discernment of spirit. They were dressed up the same way, my brothers and sisters, who would not leave home without it!

Be a spiritualistic, militaristic trooper. Keep your guard up and your sword of the Spirit in hand and you will find that you can hold back all the forces of hellishness that are around us today.

The armour is lightweight, yet dent-proof; it is invisible, yet impenetrable; it is wearable for warring purposes, but will never wear out. It is a prerequisite for stepping out of the house for anything because it righteously prepares you for everything. It is not shiney armour, therefore it will never rust out. It has flexibility so that you can always be on the move (your feet properly shod or shoed), pressing forward with never a backward look, being shielded by your faith. You are unbeatable due to the fact that there is no break in the armour that can be breached. Can't you feel the strength of the Lord and the power of His might, right now?

For a Christian to go out unprepared spiritually would be like "the emperor wearing his new clothes," like nothing at all. We must not go out without our armour. We are the children of the King . . . Let's act like it!

5

God is Good All the Time

Kent and I had returned from Texas where we visited with all our children, all our grandchildren but one and our great granddaughters. Years of prayer have gone into each one of them.

After a week of praying earnestly that God would intervene with Kent's condition, we got to go on vacation that year. God's timing was wonderful. Kent had a reaction to a medication that gave him a severe sensitivity to light. His eyes were affected to the point that he wore two sets of sunshades in the house in the darkest room possible. He went to the VA community clinic practitioner and she told him to go to an eye doctor who told him that it was not his eyes, but the medication. He had his suspicions and stopped taking the medication on Monday and saw the eye specialist on Thursday.

The Lord stepped in and by the next Tuesday, we were on our way. We had seriously considered not going to Texas that year, and had things not changed, we would have stayed in Tennessee.

It is amazing how the enemy (the Devil), would squash our

hopes and dreams. There is always opposition to the blessings of God. If Satan could destroy all glimmers of hope and
cause us to live in darkness and despair he would. I know
God has been battling for us and we put a lot of prayer and
planning in the ministry of love to our kids.

How many journeys did the prophets and pastors and preachers make and how many prayers did they pray for those they
loved? How seriously they did spread God's love! Sixty-six
books in the Bible tie in with each other and reveal a thread
that runs true throughout—revealing the love of God.

There were trips that Paul, Peter, James and John and
many others made in the early Church to share the love.
God spread His Word through the prophets of Old and the
apostles of New, who walked with Christ Himself. They all
had to walk the walk that they talked.

The Gospel is shared from day to day with walkers and
talkers around us every day. We need to listen as they tell
us the "Old, Old Story".

We all love our families. Yours may be right down the
road, ours live in Texas. Yes, we live here and ours are long
distance "prayer receivers." God cares about the family, all
families to become a part of His family. He ordained family and wants to hold every family in His all-caring hands.

Sometimes within the family, there are times to be silent

and there are times to speak. I saw that the Lord had made a way for Kent and me to see progress in the lives of our kids. God filled our hearts with a new vigor to press on in praying for their souls.

Galatians 6:9 says, *"Be not weary in well doing: for in due season we shall reap, if we faint not"*. The Word of God promises that our whole household will be saved. I stand on these words.

I don't want one of our kids lost in the shuffle when it comes time to leave this old world. I am looking forward to being with the Lord, but I want to have all of the kids there in that great reunion when we see Jesus in all His glory.

Remember that *"For God so loved the world that He gave..."* Christ didn't quit going up that hill to Calvary because He knew that His Father had a plan for all mankind. He was the Sacrifice for our sins. He knew He would die for us, stumbling and falling time and again under the load of our sin, but He hung in there to hang on a cruel tree. He did ask for His Father to let this cup pass from Him, but He didn't run and hide from the plan God had for His life to free us.

God was good enough to look ahead to a time such as this to be merciful to His people who are surrounded by such a mess. We are an abundantly blessed people who have the opportunity to believe and just await the coming of the Lord.

19

We saw our personal family. We were given a sweet trip and health to make it. God gave us strength to be strong before the kids and the grandchildren and the little great grandchildren. Of course that trip was when we only had one great granddaughter. The God of Kent and I is so full of love and mercy, we are truly blessed by our Heavenly Father. I say, "The God of Abraham, Isaac and David—He is our AWESOME GOD!"

6

God Wrote the Book

As you have noticed, I enjoy writing and have been doing so for some time. I started some 30 years ago. It does something to my very heart to put pen to paper and lift up the Lord with my words.

I consider the opportunity to do these articles a blessing beyond any expectation I could have imagined. My words are from my heart and show what the Lord has done for me and others I have known. I have written to each of you for over three years now.

I guess I'm getting more adventuresome. I started with the newspaper to write once a month. Then, it was up to twice a month and now every week [this was in 2010]. People ask me at work, where do you get the energy and inspiration to write weekly? God inclines his servants to do certain things for the Kingdom's sake. I'm writing this short section of this article to encourage others to try some area of endeavor that they at one time thought to be an impossibility. When you make yourself available, He gives anointed ability. If you have an urge, give it a shot. If God is in it, you will know it right away. (I wrote for the Herald Citizen in Cookeville, Tennessee for 7 years until we moved to Crossville.)

So, now, I'm going from giant steps, to a leap of faith. I have been writing a book for almost a year and find there are many obstacles to overcome. I tried to make it easy on myself. It is a biography of an outstanding Christian worker in our area. It is an enormous effort, I found out. My conclusion is that it is far easier to read a book than to write one! Of course, with the end in sight, I feel a deep sense of accomplishment; it will be released soon. I want to be an encourager. The encouragement is there for me to start another one of greater magnitude. See how it works? One thing leads to another and we know who our Inspiration is.

The short time I have written a book is nothing compared to the Book that God wrote. He used dozens of writers and it is made up of 66 books. The Old Testament and the New Testament are both essential to each other and confirm and back each other up, with infinite agreement of all the writers over 1500 years, from Moses the Patriach to John the Revelator.

God loves to communicate with us whether in prayer, dreams or, most essentially, in the written Word. His Word does not come back empty. *Isaiah 55:11* says, *"So shall my word be that goeth forth out of my mouth: it shall not return unto me void, but it shall accomplish that which I please, and it shall prosper in the thing whereto I sent it."*

God is a loving God and He wants to be in fellowship with us. He taught through His Son, Jesus, in the New Testament with parables which we could understand and relate to. He wants us to know His heart, He wants us to know His plan for our lives.

He has a plan for each of our lives. In *Jeremiah 29:11*, He says through Jeremiah on paper, *"I know the thoughts that I think toward you, saith the Lord, thoughts of peace, and not of evil, to give you an expected end."*

He gave us His Word (the Bible), as we know it, to tell us what His plans are for us. He tells us what is going to happen and helps us to learn from what has happened in the past.

The Bible is a love letter to us. He is telling us what to do and what not to do for our benefit. He made a blueprint for our lives. He doesn't want us to experience the pitfalls that others did in the past and wants to spare us a heart full of pain. He wants to draw us closer to Him and spare us an eternity in Hell for transgressions we have committed. He made a way of escape for our very souls and has revealed it in the pages of His Book (the Bible).

In *John 3:2*, God told us, *"Beloved, I wish above all things that thou mayest prosper and be in health, even as your soul prospereth."*

God's Words are everlasting to everlasting. He is the Alpha and the Omega. He is the Beginning and the Ending of all things! He is the "Almighty God."

I don't know everything, by any means. I do know I have experienced God's love and His mercy at work in my life and if He can do the things He has done for me—He can do it for you.

Yes, He wrote the Book that encourages my heart and keeps me strong enough to make it from day to day. He puts the smile on my face and when that smile is a little dim, He still loves me and helps me through.

His Word brings life to keep us from death. He warns us of the dangers of not being obedient to Him and His Word. In *John 15:7*, Jesus said, *"If ye abide in me, and my words abide in you, ye shall ask what ye will, and it shall be done unto you."*

I, personally, cannot make it without the Lord. My life would be a shambles without Him. This past year would have taken a far worse toll on my life with Kent's illnesses without the comfort of the God of all creation.

Yes, He wrote the Book of all books. He is the starter and finisher of all things. It is up to us to listen and stay close to Him as this world turns each day and we face more twists..

He is the greatest author Who wrote the book for all ages through the ages as the Ageless One. I haven't scratched the surface. I am grateful that God loved us enough to send His Son to die for us and that He wrote us of His love in a Book. You may not believe it, but He addressed it to you. Oh, He knows who you are; He recognizes you. He wants you to read His Word and recognize Him!

7

He Lived to Die and Lived to Die to Live Again

I have been thinking about this intriguing subject for a long time. There is a deep theological thought to this whole theme. If I succeed at what I'm aiming for, we will come to an exceedingly helpful conclusion that may change your way of thinking. Who was this man who lived and died and lived and died to live again?

It is a New Testament story involving Jesus and three of His followers. It reads like this: *"Now a certain man was sick, named Lazarus, of Bethany, the town of Mary and her sister Martha. (It was that Mary which anointed the Lord with ointment, and wiped his feet with her hair, whose brother Lazarus was sick.)* in verses *John 11:1-2.*

In this Scripture reference of *John 11:1-44*, the sisters of Lazarus sent word to the Lord that he was sick. They referred to Lazarus as *"he whom thou lovest"* when sending word to Jesus of his sickness.

Now, all three were His followers. But, there is more to this than that. Every time Jesus passed through the area, He literally stopped in. They were His closest of friends. He didn't have to send a messenger ahead of time to announce His soon arrival. They were ready to welcome Him into their home at any time.

The response of Jesus was that this was *"not unto death, but for the glory of God, that the Son of God might be glorified thereby."*

Jesus dearly loved all three, Mary, Martha and Lazarus. He stayed two days where He was, after hearing of the sickness of Lazarus.

In *verse 11*, Jesus said that their friend, Lazarus was sleeping, but He, Jesus, would go that He might awaken him. The disciples didn't understand when Jesus spoke of Lazarus as sleeping. Jesus responded by telling them Lazarus was dead and they were going to see him and his family.

When they got there, Lazarus had lain in the grave for four days already.

Martha met Jesus with the statement that had He (Jesus), been there Lazarus would not have died; but she said, she knew that whatever Jesus asked even then after four days, God would give it to Him. Think about the tremendous confidence that Martha had in Jesus and the complete confidence that Jesus had in Himself as the Immaculate Pro-Lifer.

In verse 22, Jesus responded with, *"Thy brother shall rise again."*

In *verses 25 -26, "Jesus said unto her, I am the resurrection, and the life: he that believeth in me, though he were dead, yet shall he live: And whosoever liveth and believeth in me shall never die. Believest thou this?"*

Her response was, *"Yes, Lord: I believe that you are the Christ, the Son of God, which should come into the world."* In *verse 32*, Mary responded as Martha had.

Jesus responded with compassion and asked where they had laid Lazarus. Then the shortest verse in the Bible, *verse 35* says, *"Jesus wept."* How powerful were those two words. As a human being, He was profoundly, physically moved by the moment; He grieved along with the other grievers—however, He was far more than being human.

Jesus groaned and asked those around to roll away the stone from the above ground gravesite. Jesus prayed and thanked His Heavenly Father for hearing him and He told His Father that He always heard Him but He made sure that those who were gathered around heard Him, too. When He finished praying, He said with a loud voice, *"Lazarus, come forth."*

Lazarus came forth wrapped from head to toe with grave clothes. Jesus called Him by name because had He only said, *"Come forth,"* all the graves would have burst open.

None of us are promised tomorrow. We might not see the sunrise or the sunset from today until tomorrow. How many die in automobile crashes or some sudden illness?

So, we see our humanity. We see Jesus' humanity. We see Lazarus' sisters' humanity. And, we see the humanity of Lazarus. Jesus proved with the resurrection of Lazarus that He is *"The Resurrection."* According to traditional history, Lazarus lived a full life (dying of old age), after his raising. Lazarus, Mary and Martha were faithful followers of Jesus, forever. They didn't understand that He was *"the resurrection and the life"* until He was crucified and buried in a similar grave to Lazarus' and raised again. Then, they were not only faithful followers but full believers, also.

So, when Lazarus was revived to walk out of those grave clothes, he eventually died again. Anytime we are healed, from death or otherwise, we will die again. Therefore, there is no such thing as a perfect healing in this life. With any healing, death will follow; we are creatures destined to die. Imagine, after Jesus' death, Lazarus realized that he will be raised again to never die. Because Jesus lives, he shall live also. Gather that thought into your innermost being and you will live with an incredible confidence that when your demise finally comes, you will live again to never die and be forever with the One Who lives forevermore—if Jesus Christ is your Savior.

Lazarus lived to die, to live to die, and live again eternally! I could live for that!

⎯⎯⎯⎯◄═══════

8

Holiness, Righteousness and the Blessing of God

This is definitely a difficult subject. As you have noticed through these few years, I have not shied away from the more controversial areas of Biblical thought. What I am trying to do is get the mind of God. That's not easy for any of us. What is encouraging is when the Bible says that we need the simplicity that is in Christ, Who is the Son of God. It's my desire, as I believe it is for many of us, to walk in an upright fashion. I am not talking about "holier than thou" that puts an idea in someone's head they are above all the rest of us, but holy in that you want to be holy as He, our Lord, is holy.

Ephesians 1:4 says, *"According as he hath chosen us in him before the foundation of the world, that we should be holy and without blame before him in love:"*

The beauty of His holiness is awesome. God and His touch on our lives brings peace throughout the percussion and presence of turmoil that many times assail us, even beat us down. When tragedy comes, the devil tries to draw us away from the Lord, but God is the God of all creation, full of love and mercy. He wants us to stay close to Him so He can take care of us. The farther we get away from Him, the longer He has to reach for us to bring us closer to Himself.

Holiness? Holiness is next to godliness. Yes, moral cleanliness is next to godliness! I know that when I put myself into the equation of an article, I am subjecting myself to scrutiny. But, I want to be involved. If I don't involve myself, I am suggesting something for you that I want to have nothing to do with. We are all in this together. Here we go: God expects holiness, godliness, righteousness and uprightness if we claim His Name. That name is Christian (Christ' ian; a reflection of Christ's character). If we are like Christ, we are like God because Christ came to Earth to reveal and reflect the nature of God. If we can be like Christ, we will be like God and that to me represents godliness.

Look at *Hebrews 1:1-3*, *"God, who at sundry times and in diverse manners spake... Hath in these last days spoken unto us by His Son,... Who being the brightness of His glory, and the express image of His person..."*

I know many of you are looking at these words and scratching your head and saying to yourself, I am reading this, but how do I do this. The answer is by accepting Jesus Christ as Savior and let Him work this out in you. He makes the difference. He makes us new. Many may be saying, I could never be holy as He is holy, but Christ can change you on the inside.

I'm not a Christian because Mama and Daddy were, I am a Christian because Jesus Christ lives in my heart and I serve Him.

Zachariah, the father of John the Baptist, prophesied in *Luke 1:74 -75* over the baby Jesus, *"That He would grant unto us, that we being delivered out of the hand of our enemies might serve Him without fear, in holiness and righteousness before Him, all the days of our life."*

Jesus was talking to John the Baptist in *Matthew 3:15* and said, *"Suffer it to be so now: for thus it becometh us to fulfill all righteousness."* When Jesus came out of the water from His baptizing by John, the Holy Spirit descended upon Him in the form of a dove.

God showed His pleasure in His Son's obedience. We might not have a dove descend upon us, but there are times that you know God has to have a big old smile on His face when we have done something that is especially pleasing to Him. Sometimes, I think He even gets a laugh out of the predicaments we get ourselves into and He speaks to us in our spirit to say that if we will listen and obey, He will pull us out.

Blessedness is another thing. I want the blessings of God on my household, on my husband, my children, grandchildren and soon to be great granddaughter. I believe *Deuteronomy 28:1-2* when it says, *"And it shall come to pass, if thou shalt hearken diligently unto the voice of the Lord thy God, to observe and to do all his command- ments which I command thee this day that the Lord thy God will set thee on high above all nations of the earth: And all these blessings shall overtake thee, if thou shalt hearken unto the voice of the Lord thy God."*

Our first great grandchild affected my prayer life. She was the "third" generation fruit of my body and as *verse 4* of the same chapter of *Deuteronomy* indicates, she is blessed as well as my children and grandchildren, in the stream-line of descendency. Of course now we have 6 great grand-daughters and we are even more blessed.

In addressing this whole subject, the final result is blessedness. I don't mean that one day in this life you'll wind up with a halo on your head for all to see, so they can say, *"Look at you."* Walking closely to God in holiness and righteousness produces an inward assurance that is unsurpassed. That is a blessing in and of itself; but the benefits that follow are in abundance. Allowing Christ to be 100% active in our hearts is the key to that kind of spiritual success. There is nothing more blessed than holiness and righteousness. That's God in you and you in God.

9

How Far Will You Go to Walk the Walk

One Monday evening after a day's work at Walmart, I went with my husband to a tent meeting called "Worship Without Walls, Redemption Tour", which was set up on the property of Faith Chapel Ministries, the site of the new Faith Chapel, on Highway 70 West, in Baxter. I've been to tent meetings around, but not experienced one for a good twenty to thirty years. My memory is fond of Biblical, evangelistic, revivalized tents through the years, but I wondered why I hadn't heard of one for years. Maybe, it is a need for today.

In this meeting, I heard the testimony of Sherry Argo, who had just returned from a "walk" that had impacted her life. She was alive with excitement over the experience. I had heard two weeks ago through the grapevine that she was going and began praying for her efforts.

It seems that Stephanie Hall, Sherry's friend who lives in Nashville, had an inoperable tumor healed by God. Her church had prayed for her healing and God had come through. She had, in return, made a commitment to do something to express her gratitude for what He had done for her and He had put in her heart to do this walk across the country.

Sherry Argo had promised her friend, Stephanie, who began her walk at Hammond Beach North Carolina, that she would meet her in Ashville, North Carolina, and walk with her to Pigeon Forge. Stephanie has committed to walk to Santa Monica, California. She has committed to go all the way with the Lord for He has gone all the way with her by healing her of an inoperable cancerous tumor.

Sherry, my friend, described her fear of taking on a mission for God. She was excited God had given her the opportunity to learn and grow and has come to understand: no fear is so great that God will not make provision.

Sherry learned fear can be conquered by faith in our Wonderful Lord Jehovah, the Mighty God, the Counselor, and Prince of Peace. The Holy Spirit of the Living God protects her in all adversity. Knowing this gives her the peace which surpasses all understanding. She said that it was as if she was in a bubble walking on air about six inches or more off the ground; nothing could shake or bother her.

33

It was the most awesome feeling that Sherry had ever encountered. She said her Bible had come alive to her. She had "lived" her very own chapters by following the Lord in this.

She used to have the argument that man wrote the Bible, man edited the Bible, but when she prays and opens her Bible now, it tells her exactly what she needs. It is the daily renewable Word of God and until she engaged it for herself there was no way she could understand it. Now Sherry's favorite expression is, *"God is Awesome and He loves every one of us!"*

As she shared the thoughts of her testimony under the tent, I saw the Holy Spirit causing her to get excited overwhelmingly. It reminded me of one woman I knew, who opened up the Word of God and when reading, was strengthened in her spirit and her life. She would take four different translations at one time to make sure she was illuminated as to what the rich thought was for her need that day.

I see that in Sherry in a time when there is not a lot of hope being heard, she has sweet anticipation and vibrance that comes from the very throne of God.

James 1:22, "Be ye doers of the Word and not hearers ony". She was being a doer. Then I thought of *Psalms 91: 11-12, "For He shall give His angels charge over thee, to keep thee in all thy ways. They shall bear thee up in their hands, lest thou dash thy foot against a stone."* God gave her the peace that

He was protecting her as she did her own "Emaeus Walk."

As Sherry and Stephanie walked, they met some others who needed prayer in their situations where they felt helpless and the two brought a new wind of the Holy Spirit with them to encourage these others. They were living, *Joshua 1:3, "Every place that the sole of your foot shall tread upon, that have I given unto you, as I said unto Moses."*

God is as real today as He was when He spoke this world into existence. How far would you go to walk the walk for our loving Heavenly Father Who can and will lead us in paths of righteousness for His namesake?

10

How Far Will You Go?

My thoughts turn to Abraham, the early Old Testament friend of God. Abraham is mentioned in the New Testament many times because of his faithfulness to God.

Abraham was well-respected, a highly successful farmer as a resident of Ur of Chaldee with a wife, maidens, servants, farmhands, much stock and vast lands.

You can see that Abraham isn't that much different than we are today, even though we are looking back for a few thousands of years (2000 B.C.). After being well established in an area, he hears from the LORD GOD. telling Abraham to uproot himself and move to a far off country to be His chosen servant to establish a nation numbered like the stars in the sky or as countless as the sand by the seashore.

We love Our Heavenly Father because we know Him. This God, Jehovah or I am, was "new" to Abraham. God had introduced Himself to Abraham late in Abraham's life.

He didn't know the route to get to this new land and knew nothing about this other region, the land of Canaan. And he knew little about this God Who was this one true God when he lived in a land where everyone around served many gods—but He trusted God.

It was a pluralistic society. The people served whatever god they could conveniently name. They made idols out of household pets or owls and various small animals. Everyone wanted their own god, whatever they could create... an imagination of their own thought. To think that one God made the heavens and the earth was a novel, almost amusing idea in that day. To his neighbors, it was an impossibility for one divine being to make everything that exists. Jeremiah the prophet declares. "*. . . art not Thou He, O LORD our God? Therefore we will wait upon [serve] Thee: for Thou hast made all these things.*" *- Jeremiah 14:22b.*

Abraham makes a bold move to leave it all to start over again. He said, *"Yes,"* to this God and went to a new land to make a new way for a new nation. He went "a far piece" to be a servant to a God that is true, living, and everlasting. My question to you is, *"How far would you go for Him?"*

God keeps His promises to the nth degree and never fails. *He is not a man that He should lie* and has gone a "far piece" for you and me by sending His Son, to die for us. Abraham also learned that God was a loving God just as we have. He provided a ram in the bush when it came to the point of sacrificing his son. Abraham was tested to the limit and passed.

If we are Christ's seed then we are God's seed; if we are God's seed then we are Abraham's seed. The Bible states in *Galatians 3:29, "And if ye be Christ's, then are ye Abraham's seed, and heirs according to the promise."*

Abraham was believing God. If Abraham had not set himself apart from the rest, a type of sanctification, we would have no example of faith. Abraham was looking for a foundation that only God could make and build *(Heb. 11:8-13)*. God had done His part and Abraham was obeying.

God has called us out to separate ourselves from worldliness, to take on His Name so others will know to Whom we belong, to demonstrate that we are available to respond to a special call to service for the sake of His Kingdom!

God spoke out, Abraham stepped out—we need to stand out. Abraham was a man of FAITH and believed the promise of the Provider. He was persuaded to embrace the unknown. The God he trusted is the same today and will help us through whatever comes.

Abraham's faith was so dramatic and so strong that it was mentioned in an outstanding way in *Romans 4* and Abraham was not merely an Old Testament character.

He was profoundly a worthwhile worshiper and so should we be.

As we look to the Lord for strength each day as Abraham did, we must be trustworthy. As we face difficulties daily, we must prove ourselves to the One true God that we are able to stand up in Him under the pressure that attempts to weigh us down.

I believed God that this land of Tennessee was a blessing waiting to happen when He led me here from Texas. I am not an Abraham, but that same faith lies in each of our hearts to trust God and follow His direction. God speaks, let us listen and say—YES!

How far would we go for Him?

11

I Can Only Imagine

"But as it is written, eye hath seen, nor ear heard, neither have entered into the heart of man, the things which God hath prepared for them that love Him. But God hath revealed unto us by his Spirit: for the Spirit searcheth all things, yea, the deep things of God."
                                        - 1 Corinthian 2:9-10

We sang a chorus in our former church quite often with the title, *"I Can Only Imagine."* I try to imagine what Heaven will be like for all of us who are fortunate enough to enter in. It is a hard thing to do. But there was a recent experience in my family that brought the whole idea home. Children can help us see when we look through their eyes. I think I see things a little clearer today.

Let me tell you about little Madison Brown who died on Saturday, May 24, 2010. The twelve year old had fought with Leukemia for eight years more or less. She was my third cousin. My mother and her great grandmother were sisters.

Her dad, Michael, retired from Exxon in his forties because he has MS. He became her caregiver full time so Karen, his wife, could work. Her brother, Austin, is a Sophomore in high school and gave her a bone marrow transplant.

Several years ago, I wrote about a young man named Stephen Brown who was electrocuted while fixing the hot tub out on the back deck. He was another relative of mine; Madison's uncle.

I said all that to bring us to the last nine days of Madison's life. For nine days prior to Madison leaving this old world, she was in and out of a coma. In her last weeks, she had told her mama that she would see her Uncle Stephen in Heaven. He would be waiting for her.

For twenty-three hours, Maddie had not spoken. Steadily by her side, her mother decided to lay down beside Maddie on Friday night. Karen asked Mike to turn on some sweet gospel music, the song playing was *I Can Only Imagine.* Maddie roused and said, *"Please turn it up."*

The Lord was preparing her and her family for her leaving and going home.

About a week before she died, Madison's Uncle Scott was vacuuming the living room at his house and the Lord spoke to him. He told Scott to go look at the picture of Stephen, his brother. The Lord spoke again and told him that He would be taking Madision (Maddie) home soon to be with Stephen.

God was preparing the whole family for her journey.

She would have peace and be in the presence of the Lord rather quickly.

Now I know God doesn't speak to all of us, but He has different ways of dealing with us to prepare us for the loss of someone here on Earth.

Many times, you hear of deathbed experiences, but those who walk with the Lord through *the valley of the shadow of death* are still blessed. Madison is another who went from this life to life with Christ in Heaven. She had an aniticipation of seeing her Uncle Stephen.

Madison had her sights set on Heaven. She could only imagine and the closer the time came for her to go she could see her Uncle Stephen, her great grandmother and great grandfather all waiting for her.

She knew enough to know that when she got to Heaven, she wouldn't hurt anymore—she was ready. She knew that she would be in the presence of Jesus Christ and our Heavenly Father. The Holy Spirit had comforted her for years through test after test, treatment after treatment to overcome the Cancer that had held her small frail body captive.

I never laid eyes on Maddie, but I will. I will see my little cousin, wholly and holy. She will not be frail and dying anymore—but healed and at peace. She had journeyed through this life with a desire for Glory. She was anticipating all the things she had heard about Heaven and those last nine days gave her a clearer view of her final destination.

She could only imagine, but the farther she got from here the closer she got to the most glorious place she would ever be, with the Creator and King of Kings. These are the words Maddie and her family heard together the night before our little girl was called home:

> *I can only imagine, when that day comes,*
> *and find myself standing in the Son.*
> *I can only imagine what my eyes shall see*
> *when Your face is before me.*
>
> *Surrounded by your glory, what will my heart feel?*
> *Will I dance for You Jesus, or in awe of You be still?*
> *Will I stand in Your presence, or to my knees will I fall?*
> *Will I sing Hallelujah, will I be able to speak at all?*
> *I can only imagine, I can only imagine when all I do*
> *is forever, forever worship you!*

Maddie doesn't have to imagine anymore...

12

In Memory of the Esh Family

Easter Sunday Morning, we went to church and on the way home we put a CD in to listen to a wonderful family group called the Esh Family. Our neighbor had loaned us the CD to familiarize ourselves with the music of the family.

As I listened to their wonderful a cappella music, my heart was overwhelmed by the fact that they were actually praising the Lord in His presence now. The CD's had been distributed throughout the country ministering to the Mennonite communities and spreading the Gospel of Jesus Christ with all the love that He could possibly put in those wonderful earthen vessels.

We did not know the Eshes nor had heard mention of their names until about a month ago and the news carried a message of tragedy. A van load of twelve was headed to Iowa for a wedding and all but three (the fiancé of one of the young ladies and two other young ladies), were family.

I am sure as they traveled their spirits were high and they were looking forward to seeing family and friends. In a matter of moments, everything changed: an eighteen wheeler came across the median and hit them head on, leaving two alive (a three year old and a five year old). The five year old has since said that on impact the family was singing.

My husband called our neighbor who is Mennonite and told her what he had heard and we began to become acquainted with a family whose whole lives were dedicated to serving the Lord and singing His praises.

As we listened to the waves of praise, my mind wandered to the thought of them standing before the throne singing the very songs that were on the CD. The title of the album was appropriately called, *"His Wondrous Love."* I could almost see each of those pictured on the back of the CD case singing for the great I AM, Himself. I could see the expressions and feel the love they were experiencing for all their labors they had done to serve the Lord.

I was told by several of the young women in our community that there was a great outpouring of love from all across the country to remember the gracious family who had so diligently served the Lord and their brothers and sisters in the music ministry.

The day before the funeral, there were some three thousand who showed up, and the day of the funeral there were far more than three thousand. [A sidenote: the caskets were handmade by fellow Mennonites.]

I am reminded of Scriptures about the saints regarding events in Heaven.

Revelation 5:8 says, "And when He [the Lamb, Who stood in the midst of the elders] had taken the book [the book sealed with seven seals that no one could look upon], the four and twenty elders fell down before the Lamb, having every one of them harps, and golden vials full of odours, which are the prayers of saints."

It looks like everyone in Heaven will be musical with their own harp! The vials in *chapter 5, verse 8* are our prayers, brothers and sisters. They are those prayers that we anguish over for our mates, our children, our friends, for whatever situation of desperation we may come in contact with and God has stored them up in precious vials.

In *Revelation 21*, Heaven or the new Jerusalem is described as *"prepared as a bride adorned for her husband."* In *verse 4*, it says *God shall wipe away all tears from their eyes. There will be no death, no sorrow or crying, no pain; everything will pass away.* In *Revelation 22:5, "There shall be no night there; and they need no candle, neither light of the sun, for the Lord God giveth them light: and they shall reign forever and ever".*

These people are experiencing *the peace of God* with no pain, no heartache and they are doing what they loved to do while they lived here on Earth with us. They are singing His praises in His presence.

45

Some of the songs the Esh family sang were: *Jehovah; This Is My Song To Thee; I Love you, Lord; Wondrous Love; Worthy Is The Lamb; There Is Joy; Whom Will You Serve; Blessed Jesus; One More Voice;* and *Twas Worth It all.* All in all there are ten beautiful songs on the CD, and they glorified God in each refrain with every note sung in unparalleled praise to the Lord; that ministered to others.

Since we have moved to Crossville, we have become close to the Mennonite Community. When they felt the pain of the loss, we felt it with them. The Mennonites here knew this Mennonite family from Kentucky personally. Let's all be that close.

We asked our neighbor how she felt about the whole incident. She readily replied, *"It's in God's hands. It happened. I accept it. We don't know why, but some good will come out of it. The family is home."*

It is hard to accept such devastating consquences with the peace of God. Lord will lead us through the valley of despair. It is in God's hands. This family is home and their faith has paid off in peace and an eternity with the Lord they served.

I never met them, but I will when I get to Heaven. How about you?

13

Intercession

The dictionary defines *intercession* as "prayer, petition, entreaty in favor of another. To *intercede* is to intervene between two parties with a view to reconciling differences."

According to the biblical topical index in the Nelson's Open Bible, *intercession* is "prayer offered in behalf of others, secures healing, averts judgment, insures deliverance, bestows blessings, obtains restoration, and encourages repentance."

I have found that as you pray for others, God steps in and works on your behalf. Praying for others takes our attention off our needs. It seems the more we pray for others the more God deals with our personal needs as well.

Time after time, people have come across our paths who need prayer and each one has needs. I can almost visualize God's hand moving in our behalf as we prayed for those others.

In the financial situations of those around us with an unemployment rate of around 10% and more in the years since this article, the physical well being of those we care for in a weak economy must be placed in the hands of the Lord and trust Him with all our hearts. For many of us, it is hard to trust the Lord for there have been many disappointments. In this physical (I've got to touch it to believe it) world, it is somewhat difficult to plead with God to just meet basic needs for those we know when there is so little available. But that's when God is most ready to step in.

I have had people tell me they were skeptical of the words I have shared with them, and then they have an epiphony that there is something to this when it becomes relevant in their lives. God deals with each of us differently, but His love is the same for all of us. He loved each one of us in such a way that—He gave the best gift of all; His Son to die for us on Calvary. Such heighth and breadth and depth of love is nearly unfathomable.

He, Jesus Christ, interceded for us in the garden with such fervor that He sweated drops of blood. He knew what He would be going through, but He didn't back down. *Luke 22:44* says, *"And being in agony, he prayed more earnestly and his sweat was, as it were, great drops of blood falling down to the ground."*

In *verse 42* Jesus said this, *"Father, if thou be willing remove this cup [suffering] from me: nevertheless not my will, but thine, be done."*

My interpretation of this is Father I don't really want to do this but I will do what You want. I know how much You love Your children.

He did the ultimate act of intercession when He (Christ), hung on the old rugged cross and bore our sins (the sins of all mankind). What a load He carried to that tree of misery; what a weight of heartache He burdened upon Himself for us.

There have been times in my life when I had to bear up under shame and heartache; and I'm sure, many of you, if not all, have experienced such pangs of discomfort. Multiply that by thousands and even millions and that is what Christ felt on the cross. If our situations pull us down and Christ went to the cross knowingly bearing all our burdens, He must have suffered tremendous pain and anguish in that time spent in the garden in preparation for His death.

Even now He is ever interceding at the right hand of the Father for us. He has not forgotten us and His ears are listening for our petitions, for our personal requests and for others. He gives us our daily bread.

There is somebody reading this script right now who is saying to himself or herself that this is "fairy tale" stuff. It is false, phoney, a farce. He is as real as you and me and what He did for us has longer lasting consequences than any contract you could ever sign on the dotted line. It will last past the need for a will to leave your earthly belongings to your children or grandchildren. Try Him . . . He'll make a believer out of you!

This is a time in history when we must cry out to the Lord in intercession for the young men and women overseas fighting for freedom for others and holding the enemy at bay in our homeland as well. We must intercede for the missionaries and doctors who carry their compassion and their talents to others in other lands across the world. We bring our petitions to the Lord and He gladly responds to protect the warriors in the foxholes and deserts, in the airships and on the battlefields and on the bases. Now with the threat of North Korea, we must pray even harder that God will catch their leaders in the trap they are setting for us. *Psalms 35:7* gives us a promise, *"For without cause have they hid for me (us) their net in a pit, which without cause they have digged for my (our) soul., (v 8) Let destruction come upon him at unawares; and let his net (the enemy's net set for us) that he hid catch himself; into that very destruction let him fall."* To me, these are our enemies who have set traps for us to destroy us individually or countries who want to destroy us.

Hebrews 7:25 speaks of Jesus, *"Wherefore He is able also to save them to the uttermost that come unto God by Him, seeing He ever liveth to make intercession for them".*

Then the next verse says, *"For such a high priest became*

us, who is holy, blameless, undefiled, separate from sinners, and made higher than the heavens." In *verse 27*, it says that He became the sacrifice and He did this once, when He offered up Himself. This is talking about His crucifixion on the cross.

We are ahead of the game of life if we trust the Lord. We are not by ourselves in our battle; we have the Lord on our side. We will be able to get victory over the enemies that assail us from day to day and fear is one of the biggest. Fear is one of Satan's strong men and it fights our faith every step of the way.

Faith in Christ will set us free from our shackles. Interceding for others while trusting God to take care of our beloved families and friends is an effectual way to reach the whole realm of needs within our immediate world is His desire for us. He (God), wants us to be ready in season and out to pray for others.

Pray for others because someone is praying for you right now. *Intercession* is an awesome tool that God has given us—hold fast and watch His hand move. When you pray for someone else for blessings, God is saying, *"Back at ya!"*

14

Let Those Who Have Ears Let Them Hear

I can't help myself. It is the same subject as last week. I feel compelled to do so.

When God calls us how do we hear Him? What would keep us from hearing Him?

There are so many voices in this world, just as there were when Peter stepped out of the boat to walk on the water with Jesus. It is as if life is becoming a major faith walk for those who trust the Lord. With all those voices pulling us to and fro and trying to convince us there is no God and that our Heavenly Father is merely a myth, how do we stay strong and trust the Lord anyhow?

We just do it. We read and pray and trust His Word above all else. We tune in to His frequency by listening to Him through His Word. *Psalms 51:10* states, *"Create a clean heart in me; and renew a right spirit within me."* I understand that there is incident after incident that causes insult and injury and brokenness and breakdown; however, there is an answer to carrying that load of pain—it's called repentance. We have no control over the things others do to us, but we do have the ability to give the bitterness back to God Who understands heartache. *"If we mend our ways, He will mold our days."*

There are times He calls me to prayer in the night or early hours of the morning. One morning, years ago, I awoke and saw one of the children off my bus route as if he were standing by my bed. His name was Jimmy Laurie. He looked ill and the Lord spoke to me to pray. I did and asked his mother the next week if something had been wrong with him and she said he had a high fever that would not break all night and then finally broke at 5:30 am. That's the time the Lord told me to pray.

Proverbs 3:5 says, *"Trust in the Lord with all thine heart; and lean not to thine own understanding. In all thy ways acknowledge Him, and He shall direct thy paths. Be not wise in thine own eyes: fear the Lord, and depart from evil. It shall be health to thy navel, and marrow to thy bones."*

If we can come to the Lord with a clean heart, we are more able to hear Him with clarity. There are the those who will tell you that when they come to the saving knowledge, the birds sing louder and the trees look greener and the sky is bluer; their lives have taken a turn for the better in a matter of seconds—they are clean inside and out. For a few, I am absolutely sure that is the case. For most of us, it is a new state of acceptance and assurance with a step by step move to a fuller, richer, deeper walk with God. You are now headed in the right direction. What you do is immediately realize that God is dealing with you and is constantly trying to tell you something in every facet of your life. God is being heard as a soft, still, sweet, small voice that you are attuned to. You are more able to hear the Lord for direction in your life because you are now turned His way.

Jimmy Laurie's mom was one of those who plunged in and received a new found relationship with Christ. It was as though everything came to life for her. She was a responder and still is.

The key to hearing and responding is a clean heart. Jesus speaks in *John 15* about our relationship to Him and in *verse 3* He says, *"Now ye are clean through the word which I have spoken unto you."* Then in *verse 4* Jesus says, *"Abide in Me, and I in you. As the branch cannot bear fruit of itself, except it abide in the vine; no more can you, except ye abide in Me."*

He is speaking to us through everyday crises to around-the-world catastrophes. Have you noticed how uneasy (on edge) everybody seems to be these days? It is as if they all are anticipating a major upheaval that will effect the whole globe. It has been my experience, that some who are not particularly religious see an "end-time" event approaching.

I've had people ask me, *"How is the world treating you?"* My response is usually, *"Not worth a flip but the Father is taking care of me."*

We must stay tuned in to the Lord for He is our *"strength*

and our shield." If we do so with a clean heart, we will hear ever so clearly. If we do not hear, we're not close enough to Him, He rarely shouts out. His Holy Spirit is a gentleman, He will not bite your head off or pull your ears out of place—He is reaching out.

Are you ready to respond? Be a ready, willing and able servant of the Savior. The outcome will exceed your imagination.

15

Listen for the Call

Sometimes, I think about all of us. Using myself as an indicator is not always reliable. I have agonized over a certain issue for years. It might have happened to you, too. I am an older woman now; to some, considerably older. My age is no tightly held secret. I am in my mid-sixties. As the body slows down, the mind quickens for some. I have learned to look behind me in reference to my past to build a more productive future.

The first call from the Lord came when I was eight years old and I remember vividly a Sunday night service when the Holy Spirit drew me as if a giant invisible hand was pulling me to come to the Lord to be saved; it was not like a physical pull, but a 'come with me' type of pulling where I had to go—I accepted the Lord that night. I didn't go because some little friend of mine was going, I experienced the touch of the Holy Spirit drawing me to make Jesus Christ my Savior.

At the age of thirteen, I felt the Lord drawing me to the mission field. I always felt I would go to deep dark Africa. I yielded myself that day to missions and began building my life around that call and my answer, *"Yes."* At one point while I was still in Texas, I went to sing in black churches, prisons, and Spanish churches, but never made it to the mission field overseas.

When I was about nineteen, I felt like the Lord wanted me to be a social worker. Again I said, *"Yes, Lord."*

Then when I was around twenty-seven years of age, I wanted to know that I was okay with the Lord. I had lost both parents by this time. My dad had just died. I was checking my foundation to see there were no cracks and nothing to keep me from Heaven. I wanted to be sure that I would see the two people who had brought me into this world and walked me through my spiritual life during my growing up years. Now I want to see Jesus first and my parents and my big brothers who have gone on to Heaven. I will get to see my two sisters and brother who died at birth.

At the age of twenty-seven, I yielded to the bus ministry at the church I attended and worked diligently for some five years in the bus ministry. Within that five years or more I brought over 5,000 children and adults to church and several of the families were saved during that time.

God calls, but do we respond? Yes, we respond, but not always with a yes. Sometimes we respond with doing absolutely nothing which is in all reality, a NO..

Later, we find out that if we had moved in a direction or called a person or even made an effort, something might have changed in the lives of countless others.

Some are called as a child and don't respond until they are older. They may have said *"Yes"* as a child, but the commitment did not come until later years.

The Bible says that many are called, but few are chosen. *Romans 11:29* says, *"For the gifts and calling of God are without repentance."*

As husbands and wives, we are called to minister to our family. As women and men who have been through turmoil in our lives, our call is to the masses who experienced the same types of problems.

Children at a younger age are able to hear the Holy Spirit and respond more readily. The older we get, the same call may be reactivated by some illness or travesty that has occurred in our lives. God is the same God when we are adults that He was when we were children and the Bible says—His call is without repentance. He is just as serious about the answer we give now to the call sent to our heart as when we were children.

I guess this is what I'm leading up to: a confession. My life has never fully fulfilled any call that God has put upon me through the years. This admission has been good for me . . . a cleansing of my spirit. And, I think that my motivation for these articles is to make up for my shortcomings in my calls to do something. This is quite fulfilling. I realize I'm reaching more people these days through these newspaper articles than at any other time in my life. They came through my Walmart register and told me so. I'm grateful.

My son told me over the years, Mama, you can't save them all. I told him I couldn't save them anyway, but I could try. So, maybe I'm catching up. That is an incredible thought to me. Do you know where I'm coming from? There may be a confession that you need to make, also. God never gets through with us . . . that goes for you, too!

16

Loss is More Often Gain

Loss of loved ones is final to many people, but to Christians it is merely a beginning of a new way of facing life. Yes, when we have lost a loved one, oftentimes we wonder why did it have to happen to that person or why now or even just why?

There was a young man named Palmer who was a dedicated Christian. He went to Maine with a church group on a mission trip. He didn't come home. His death was quick and unexpected and his whole life had been ahead of him.

I have heard that he was a sincere young believer. He was an honor student and dedicated to the cause of Christ. I didn't know him personally, but just the faith I heard about was enough to mention.

Yes, we have been losing many loved ones lately, but there is a Scripture that gives us hope. This Scripture speaks to me of the preparation that God has done (in making a way) for us to see our loved ones again.

Young people have been shot in school because of their belief in Christ. Columbine in Colorado was one, and then more recently the group called Isis has killed people throughout our country.

In *II Corinthians 4:7-10, "But we have this treasure in earthen vessels, that the excellency of the power may be of God, and not of us. We are troubled on every side, yet not distressed; we are perplexed, but not in despair; Persecuted, but not forsaken; cast down, but not destroyed; Always bearing about in the body the dying of the Lord Jesus, that the life also of Jesus might be made manifest in our body. For we which live are always delivered unto death for Jesus' sake, that the life also of Jesus might be made manifest in our mortal flesh."*

This young man, Palmer, lived a short life, but a life that shouted to the rafters of the love of Jesus Christ in him. There have been many who saw his life lived before them. I was told of his testimony and that he walked honestly and uprightly before the Lord. There will be many who will miss him and his shining light that revealed what Christ was doing in his life.

I am amazed at the wonders of God in the lives of His children. I am blessed to know His people and although some lives are short lived and others are long lived, God has made a way for these earthen vessels that we live in to be with Him. We bear the precious seed that has been planted in our souls, as did Palmer and when a life ends we have the promise of a reunion in Heaven.

Palmer had the freedom to witness without the condemnation many of our brothers and sisters in other lands are having to face, but he shared the same love they do.

He was free to live his life as a Christian and experience God's infinite mercy which is unending and everlasting. The power of God is the same that it was in the days Jesus walked this earth.

There are those who share the same faith we do who are troubled on every side and just to be able to worship, they have to meet in secret. We are not forsaken and we have been *"delivered unto death for Jesus' sake"* as the Scripture mentions. There are those who have been forbidden to live as a Christian and are threatened with their very lives.

The pain experienced by those who have lost loved ones is the same throughout mankind. If we look to the Lord, He will give those who have had great loss the peace they need to make it through. He cares about our pain and He defends His children.

God is still at work and He will bless Palmer's short life with a harvest of souls. He watched this young man's life closely, and so did those who were his family, friends, congregation, and acquaintances. Loss is gain in such situations. We are grieved because we will not see these loved ones until we get to Heaven, but in the meantime we can draw close to the Lord and invest in our future in Christ so that we will have a wonderful reunion with our precious ones.

When someone loves the Lord, their lives may be the only Bible that some read. Some who know these precious people who go to be in the presence of the Lord may not be Christians, but come to know and accept Christ as Savior. We must sow and plant for we never know who is watching or listening.

Again and again, we find that God's ways are not our ways. What is meant for evil will be turned to good. We are flesh and God is Spirit. What is spirit is not always according to the flesh, the two war against each other. Holiness is not what our flesh wants, but the Holiness of God is for us to be more like Him and drawing closer to Him. Eventually, our ultimate destination is Palmer's, Heaven and home. If we know the Lord, we will go to Heaven and the loss of our loved ones becomes gain. We now have a prize, a treasure laid up for us. We have that hope, because Jesus Christ has given us the opportunity to see our loved ones again. Loss is gain when it comes to Heaven.

17

Snatch Them From the Jaws of Hell

Over the years, I have made contact with many people. I have prayed with an immeasurable number of people and I still see the needs of those around me.

Our commandment is *"Go and Tell"* in the New Testament. That commandment is in *Matthew 28:18-20, "And Jesus came and spake unto them, saying, All power is given unto Me in heaven and in earth. Go ye therefore, and teach all nations, baptizing them in the name of the Father, and of the Son, and of the Holy Ghost: Teaching them to observe all things whatsoever I have commanded you: and, lo, I am with you always, even unto the end of the world. Amen."*

This has sent Christian missionaries throughout the world for centuries. This is why they have traveled to the Middle East, to Africa, the islands in the sea and *"to the uttermost parts of the world."* God doesn't want one to be lost. The only way souls will be lost is by their own choice and not accepting Christ as Savior. It is not because He has not made provision for them. That provision was and still is Jesus Christ, our Savior.

God is a passionate, sensitive and loving God, not a god made of stone, wood or even plastic, which has no answer when you call. God is a merciful, forgiving God Who cares what happens to us and all of our sons and daughters, as His children. He cares what happens to each of us; He wants to infold all of us into His everlasting arms of infinite care. He wants us to walk in obedience to His statutes. If we do, He will bless us according to *Deuteronomy 28:1-14;* but then if we are disobedient, there are curses in store as listed in the rest of the same chapter.

There are those who can tell you that when they served the

devil and were out there in the world, they fought hard and played hard, but once they came to a saving knowledge of Jesus Christ, they are now hardy and hearty soldiers for the Lord. They have experienced the presence of a sweet Savior touching their hearts and turning those hearts of stone to flesh.

It's all about finding a new "WAY" where men and women who have been snatched from the jaws of Hell want to show others this same way—a way out of *"gloom, despair and agony on me"*.

There is such a thing as *"flash in the pan religion."* It doesn't really last, but then there is that bonafide *"Born Again"* experience which totally transforms with a new life plugged into a heavenly place. It is hard for an unbeliever to witness such a thing and not say, *"Something has happened to you. I don't know what it is, but it has been dramatic. You are not the same person. You have really changed. What in the world is going on?"*

Well, the answer is not so complicated. We can't fix ourselves, but we have found One Who can! Christ is the life-changer; He opens the heart, eyes, ears and the hands to be a giver rather than a taker.

There is such a thing as "jailhouse" religion and it lasts only as long as they are held captive. When they are freed, they free themselves for all their jail clothes and religious clothes. But, then there are some who get saved while in jail and learn that they have been freed from captivity and Hell with all of its consequences. This comes from a reality that God is bigger than all their sin and He is their *"Buddy" throughout the rest of their life to be their "WAY."*

When a person accepts Christ, they become like new in their spirit. In God's eyes, it is as if they had never sinned. It's as if they were as innocent as a new born baby. When they accept Christ, they are covered by the blood. It doesn't matter if they were murderers, prostitutes, drunks, druggies, each one is savable. You are currently saved from the power of sin and one day, saved from the penalty of sin, HELL.

When saved, surroundings are still the same and maybe circumstances, however, the help is available that has never been there before. This new born again babe in the Lord has more possiblity than they ever had. However, things appear brand new, the trees, leaves, the sound of creation singing praises to God.

When the disciples asked Jesus about Hell, He told them that the fires of Hell were seven times hotter than Gehenna which was a burning ground for trash outside the city of Jerusalem. Hell is a place where one relives their shortcomings over and over and the flesh is not burned up. It is unending torture, just as we have eternal life as Christians and no tears and heartaches, no death and no pain.

Let's not lose even one to the gaping jaws of Hell, but lead them to a saving knowledge of Jesus Christ. We want victors instead of victims. We want them to be overcomers. Hell is awful and we all get an idea how bad it is by all the hellish things that happen to us on this side of Heaven and Hell. Get to know Jesus and get far away from even the nipping of those jaws at your heels, because—Hell is not one big party.

Hell isn't preached a lot anymore, but it's real and there will be no parties down there as some imply when joking around. But it's no joke. The thought should scare the hell out of you!

18

The Plan for Our Lives

Jeremiah 29:11 says, *"For I know the thought that I think to-ward you, saith the Lord, thoughts of peace and not of evil, to give you an expected end."* Another translation says, *"I know the plans I have for your life."*

In *Genesis*, God saw how things were turning when sin came to abide in the earth. I had a pair of friends in the Garden of Eden, Adam and Eve, who chose to disobey. God had given them food and everything they needed, but the Tree of Knowledge was their downfall. God said you can have everything but that and they had tried it anyway.

Of course, Satan showed up in the form of a beautiful serpent on two legs. He convinced Eve to try the fruit of the tree of Knowledge in the midst of the Garden. She tasted the fruit and realized she was naked and knew more than she had ever known before. Then she introduced Adam to this amazing fruit and when it came time to answer to God her response was something to the effect, *"the devil made me do it"*.

Rebellion, sin and "let's not listen to God" had arrived on Earth. Now was the time for the plan to come into action. It shows our right to free wills when Adam and Eve were planted in Paradise.

God had the plan of all plans. He would give the best thing He had to vindicate man. He would give His most prized possession at the right time.

There were many forerunners (prophets) to teach and to tell people of God's love. The last of which was John, The Baptist. Finally, He had to bring out His secret weapon, Plan B, "B" standing for Blessing!

"But with the precious blood of Christ, as of a lamb without blemish and without spot: Who verily was foreordained before the foundation of the world, but was manifest in these last times for you... "
- I Peter 1:19-20

Jesus Christ became the sacrifice to purchase our redemption from sin, to buy us back from the clutches of the enemy of our souls. Yes, we are born into sin through Adam, the first offender, but there is an answer for the sinful state for everyone. That answer is accepting Jesus Christ.

Christ bore the stripes of a cat-of-nine tails. It was not merely leather strips, but strips with pieces of metal in the ends of each piece, the Roman way in those days. It dug into His flesh and ripped it open. He bore those stripes for our physical healing.

The Lamb of God, Jesus, wore a crown woven of thorns. The thorns were not like those on a briar bush, but thorns that were a couple of inches or more, kind of like black locust thorns. This crown was jammed into His brow to heal us of any mental disorders. He bore all this pain for us.

He hung on the cross and bore the weight of our sins billions of times over, for the people who lived then and all that have lived since.

Many of you have heard these things for years and have gotten tired of hearing it, but Mom and Dad taught you and loved you. Some of our parents hammered it at us and some didn't stress it enough, but Jesus Christ stepped in front of that "long black train" for us when He hung on that cross.

Now another Easter approaches and we are reminded that

Christ died and rose again. He is the second Adam as it says in *1 Corinthians 15:20-23: "But now is Christ risen from the dead, and become the first fruits of them that slept (died). For since by man came death, by man came also the resurrection of the dead. For as in Adam all die, even so in Christ shall all be made alive."*

When Christ arose, He was the first fruit of the new covenant God made with man. That is why it is called the "New" Testament. God gave us a way as believers to live again. Death is not all there is.

It is as if Jesus is standing at the door. He is waiting for the moment that God's archangel will sound the trumpet to signal Jesus to make a second appearance on Earth for the final conclusion of the ages.

May we honor and praise the Lord for all He has done and all that He wants for us this Easter. It is not His plan we should perish, but that we should live through the power of His resurrection. It is also His desire for us to live with Him in glory. Jesus is the key to everlasting life. That's God's plan for you.

Now, for the rest of *I Peter 1:19-21: " . . . was manifest (revealed) in these last times for you, who by Him do believe in God, that raised Him up from the dead, and gave Him glory: that your faith and hope might be in God."*

You may have a picture of what you could be and you don't see yourself living up to that person you see. God has a plan for your life and only Christ holds the key to what you can be in that plan. Step up and into the plan our heavenly Father has for you. You don't have to dream anymore, but you can be all you can be in the Lord.

He knows the plan He has for you.

19

To Everything There is a Season

The leaves are changing colors and this year we have had a rough ride with hurricanes in Texas and Florida, with more to come. They are getting ready to fall. During the winter, trees, bushes and perennial flowers will lie dormant and rest until growing season.

It will soon be Thanksgiving, then Christmas and soon Easter and Spring will be knocking at our door. God knew what He was doing when He created this world in the perfect balance within which it revolves. He knew all that we would need to survive. He spoke the sun, moon and stars into existence.

All of that reminds me of the past memories of Thanksgiving and Christmas. I remember my mom would have a wonderful table set with turkey and dressing, potato salad, green beans, beautiful desserts and a bundle of love invested in all the fixings she had prepared.

I know there were times when things weren't so available for a wonderful meal, but our families would do with what they had and lack was never noticeable. Mama talked about how they made it through rough times and they knew it was the hand of the Lord.

Our parents and grandparents didn't have a lot during the Great Depression, but they had their faith and prayer to fellowship with our Heavenly Father. The mothers would stir that soup or pot of beans and pray. The fathers would plow the fields and pray. They invested in their families from their hearts.

How many of you remember a praying grandmaw who told you about what God could do for you? Do you remember the labors of her hands preparing special things for you when you went to see her? It may have even been a Sunday dinner.

Some of my cousins told my mom that she was the best chicken cooker and cake cooker they had ever known. Of course, they are all grown and have their own lives now. The memories of those who have blessed us with their touch to help us grow in the Lord, come back at special times of the year. I am sure there are some bad memories that are not as enjoyable to remember, but those family get togethers are special.

I hope that I have some good memories to leave with my grandchildren and great grandchildren. When I have a chance to speak to them, I always remind them that I am praying for them. If they have a problem, I pray for them whether they know it or not. I pray when I don't know what is going on with them.

I don't remember going to Nacogdoches at Christmas, but I do remember going and visiting grandmaw at times and putting my feet under her old antique table with claw feet. She would fix biscuits, homemade sausage and home grown eggs. Sometimes she would warn me not to drink the milk because the cow had gotten into bitterweed.

We have a lot to give thanks for each year throughout the Christmas and New Year holidays. We have a heritage of loving people who have prayed for us. If you do not have that heritage, your Heavenly Father loves you and He desires to give you that heritage of love. I know there are those who don't know who their parents are, but the adoption by the blood of Jesus Christ can appease that gnawing desire to know where we came from and who our parents are.

There is a season to everything, Christmas, Thanksgiving, and all those memories make up the sum total of who we are. Maybe you don't have a lot of memories, but you are precious in the sight of God.

Even more important than the season of Thanksgiving or Christmas is the time of history, this season that we are walking through. I pray that I am found with the type of faith that is needed to face all of the many situations that our country faces. I pray we can walk in the strength of the faith of our forefathers, even the strength of the young psalmist, David, as he faced the lion and bear to protect his flock of sheep and then the giant, Goliath, with five smooth stones.

We must stand in the faith of our fathers, even greater faith than theirs for such a time as this. The Holy Spirit is brooding over the face of the deep of our hearts as He did when He brooded over the face of the deep to create the world in the beginning.

There is a time and season for everything, birth, death, joy and sadness. God knows our hearts' desires and He knows the time it should all happen. What an awesome loving God.

20

Use It and It Grows

I ask in this manner because my husband is always picking at me for responding to him with *"What now?"* or *"Do what?"* When I genuinely fail to hear what he has just said. When someone says that all I talk about is faith, it is because—FAITH is important in our lives.

The word *'faith'* is thrown around casually among religious circles, especially amongst theologians and academians; but faith is practiced everyday by all of us. When you go to bed at night you expect (believe, have faith) that you will get up the next morning. When you get into your car for your daily rounds, you have faith that it will start up, get you there and back. When you finally get home at the end of the day, you have faith that your home (house, apartment, abode) will be there. You place a stamp on an envelope and you expect it to get to its destination. You send an E-mail and you believe it will reach the party at the other end. Notice that in these instances and in endless other examples, a doubt never enters your mind that it will be so. I would venture to say that our faith is what gets us through the tedious difficulties of everyday living. That is exercising a little bit of faith in a lot of things.

Worry is not faith and tears our faith down. It ties the hands of God and so does fear.

Faith is simple, but subtle. It is subtle, but sophisticated. You have faith in something or you wouldn't get out of bed in the morning. Why not take your simple faith and magnify it to a degree that your faith rests in the Faithful One? Why not let your "little" faith become a "larger" faith to a "larger than life" faith where it rests on something that is larger than life, itself.

It is a matter of what or who you put your faith in that makes a difference. Without this intangible item called faith, we cannot please God. Some of us trust in our big fine cars or beautiful strong houses, but when a tornado comes through it can become a pile of matchsticks.

Hebrews 10:38-39 says, "Now the just shall live by faith: but if any man draw back, My soul shall have no pleasure in him. But we are not of them who draw back unto perdition [destruction]; but of them that believe [have faith] to the saving of the soul."

There is a Hall Of Fame of men who believed and put their faith in God. It is in *Hebrews 11* right behind the definition of faith. Remember that *"by faith the elders [the Old Testament believers] obtained a good report." (Heb. 11:2)*

In Hebrews the list includes: Abel, Enoch, Noah, Abraham and Sarah, Isaac, Jacob, Joseph, Moses' parents, Moses, Joshua and Rahab and many others who are called the "Heroes of Faith."

John 14:12-14 says, "Verily, verily, I say unto you, He that believeth on me, the works that I do shall he do also; and greater works than these shall he do; because I go unto my Father. And whatsoever ye shall ask in my name, that I will do, that the Father may be glorified in the Son. If ye shall ask any thing in my name, I will do it."

Jesus is speaking in that Scripture to us. I have come to realize that it is possible to do greater than He had done while here on Earth because He went to the Father and the Father sent us His Spirit [the Comforter, the Encourager, the Enlightener, the Helper, the Empowerer, the Teacher, the Faith Builder-*John 14:26]* to make us magnifiers of His LOVE, in us through His Holy Spirit, love can abound! The God-Man Jesus gave it to man. Now, it goes from man to man or woman to woman, until it reaches the masses. Jesus only reached the area of Judea; but, we are reaching the world, one man or woman, boy or girl at a time. It is by this kind of faith that we please God.

In this same section of Scripture, Judas (not Iscariot) asked Jesus, *"...Lord, how is it that Thou wilt manifest [disclose] Thyself unto us, and not unto the world? Jesus answered and said unto him, If a man love Me, he will keep My words: and My Father will love him, and We will come unto him [through the Spirit], and make Our abode with [live within] him." (John 14:22-23)* In this Twenty-First Century we can be "super heroes" of faith.

With ever-widening, individual faith we can reach the world. So, we went from the little faith in your little world to the largest faith in the larger world. Oh, you don't have that kind of faith? Jesus believed in you for that kind of faith. Greater than He did, can we do! Jesus said so!

Let me challenge you. We have all heard about little ol'

Jabez in *I Chronicles 4:9-10*. Only two verses of Scriptures. This is all we know about him. He stood out with God. He was more notable than his brethren. He prayed a simple prayer. *He called on the God of Israel to ask, "Oh that Thou wouldst bless me indeed, and enlarge my coast [my territory, my faith], . . . And God granted that which he requested."* That was a simple prayer with solid results.

"Do what" with faith? Faith is *"what now"*? It is vital to our lives—exercise it, expand it, enlarge it; go from faith to Faith to FAITH! One step then another and you will grow in faith, God will increase your faith, He will increase your strength in Him from faith to Faith to FAITH!

21

What's the Difference?

In *Ezekiel 44,* God's Word is talking about the qualifications of the temple priests. We would call them pastors or preachers. *Verse 23* says, *"And they shall teach my people the difference between the holy and profane, and cause them to discern between the unclean and the clean."*

Malachi 2:7 says, *"For the priest's lips should keep knowledge, and they should seek the law at his mouth: for he is the messenger of the Lord of hosts."*

Again in *Leviticus 10:10* it says, *"And ye may put difference between holy and unholy, and between unclean and clean."*

If I hear these Scriptures with clarity, there is a difference in right and wrong and the people of God are to live a life that demonstrates a difference. *"Know the difference, show the difference and make the difference."* The pastors and preachers, evangelists and Sunday School teachers are supposed to teach that we are to make a difference, thus, by being different.

Paul says in *II Corinthians 6:17, "Wherefore come out from among them, and be ye separate, saith the Lord and touch not the unclean thing and I will receive you."*

This is how the Lord would have us carry ourselves. It is not to say that we walk with our nose in the air, but that we walk in a virtuous way to indicate a higher, holy walk. People need to see a difference in our lives. If they can see the Lord making us a constant work in progress and see something of value that can't be thrown aside, others on the outside looking in may realize God can do the similar and superior things for them.

I know I talk a lot about our kids and grand kids, but that is our legacy. What are we leaving them if we are doing the same thing the worldly do? Yes, even Christians make mistakes, but there is always someone watching, so be careful. There are little eyes watching us to see how we are handling our everyday life.

Children came through my line at Walmart and they watched their moms and dads like hawks to be helpful to grow up faster, like get the bags or push the buttons on the credit card machine. They want to do the things they see mom and dad doing and how many other things are they watching that have more substantial consequence? What do they see us doing or hear us saying?

I'm sure you have heard it said, *"Don't do as I do, do as I say do."* That's the way we don't want to live our lives, I tell you without a doubt! Doesn't that create a moral quandary in the person to whom it was spoken? When you see your parent doing one thing and telling you not to do it, what are you thinking? They're being told to do one thing and what their mentors are doing is totally the opposite. *"You can't have a disciple without being an example."* How can kids grow up and live a stable life when they are taught two different ways?

In *Isaiah 5:20* says, *"Woe unto them that call evil good, and good evil: that put darkness for light, and light for darkness: that put bitter for sweet, and sweet for bitterness."* In God's mind, if you are distinctive, you are distinguished.

We hear a lot of things in the world today that say it is okay to do wrong and not okay to do good. We hear of child abuse. Recently, I saw on the news that a seven year old boy was killed by his father and step mother and fed to the pigs. What was the example that man's father showed him? Another story showed a five year old girl who had been starved and kept in a closet. We have heard things like this over the years, but it seems to be more frequent. Then we hear of abortion and the horrible way babies are pulled from their mother's wombs.

The reasoning is that everybody is doing the wrong so it can't be so wrong and forget about doing good because no good deed goes unpunished. You hear the words of the world telling you that very thing, that evil is good and good is evil.

The thing that I understand in my heart and mind is— God has not changed; His morals and values have not changed. Just because the times and the thoughts of the populous change, it seems to dictate what we think we should do that would compromise the teaching of God's Holy Word. We still need to stand up for the Lord and then walk straight. We ought not to be wishy washy, milk-toast, namby-pamby, swept up by every wind of doctrine, wimpy-limpy, like a Chameleon lizard, backing down to blend in, half-hearted, lukewarm, jelly-spined, playing the victim card when we should be victor, standing in the fringes instead of jumping into the fray, afraid to wear the T-shirt that says, "I'm One of Them."

The Lord and His leadership in our lives make the difference. Then the results do not leave people wondering as to whose side are we on? To many, the word 'Christian' leaves a bad taste in their mouths because they have seen those who claim to be Christians do evil. Trusting in the Lord is the difference in success or failure; that difference then changes us and also has a chance of changing others. Those around us see God is doing something awesome and that is attractive to them. By being different (as different as Light is from darkness)—you will make a difference.

The children are our future and we must set the example for them. I once worked in a grocery store in Texas and when I went to the booth for change, the young woman working there that day said, *"You are always smiling, doesn't anything bother you?"* I said, *"Sure, but I put it in God's hands."*

Excuse me from getting a little stirred up. There was a little extra emotional intensity inside of me. I don't mind leading the way because we are open books being read all the time. When they read me, I want them to be reading "THE WORD."

I want them to see the love of Christ and His peace in me. I don't put on a smile, it is just there and I want to be an example for anyone and everyone I see. I have not been perfect in my life, but Christ in me is Who helps me through this life; He is our example. He is the difference in my life and the difference in the lives of many sold out Christians who have been brought from the darkness into the light.

22

Where Does This Stuff Come From?

You know, we who are Christians love the Word of God and try to read it regularly. One of our great consternations is that we can't remember it word for word or remember concise thoughts when we need it in the midst of casual conversation. It would have made a substantial point within the conversation, but our mind failed us. Well, don't you worry your head about it. In everyday conversation you are using the Word without knowing it, probably. I'm going to give you a couple dozen out of hundreds in the Bible. You really are a Bible quoter and don't know it. It just shows how God's great Word has permeated our society in daily talking. Praise God! We are a Christian nation!

Here is what you have heard or you have said yourself, without knowing where it came from: *"I'm getting ready to move my stuff"* or *"Give me my stuff." (Ezekiel 12:3-7)* Ezekiel is telling the children of Israel that they are going into exile and when they move out they had better take their "stuff" with them.

"I know this is odd, but when I write it on the palm of my hand, I remember it." Isaiah 44:5. God asks those that are His to write His Name on their hand.

"Surely folks have been writing on their hands for a long time; I'm not the only one I've seen do it." (Isaiah 49:16) God even wrote on his hands to remember those that are His. Obviously, it was the custom of the times, meaning that if you inscribe something in the palm of your hand, in this case God did both hands for emphasis, you plan to remember for a long time, if not forever, what is written thereon. If you are looking up the scriptures (I certainly hope you are) a follow-up to this is *Isaiah 49:22* in which God says He will lift up that name on His hand to the Gentiles as a "standard."

"Where did you hear that?" "A little bird told me!" (Ecclesiastes 10:20) The preacher *(Ecclesiastes)* states that people from the king to the rich shall receive their messages from "a bird of the air." It shall be "winged" to you.

"Try putting out the fleece; it may give you the answer." (Judges 6:37-40) The Judge to the Israelites, Gideon, asked God to give him a sign when he put a coat of wool (the fleece) on the ground ovenight.

"You did the good Samaritan thing." (Luke 10:30-37) Jesus gives us the parable (teaching tool) where He indicates that when you do something simply out of compassion, such as the original "Samaritan who did good," when he took in a man who had fallen among thieves, stripped and wounded, when no one else who passed by would. The term "neighborly" comes from the last verse in that Scripture. Another footnote: The term "half dead" like when we

say, *"you're walking around as if you're half dead,"* is derived from that same scriptural reference.

"That's impossible. That would be like going through the eye of a needle." In *Matthew 19:24*, Jesus was implying that it is impossible for a camel to go through *"the eye of a needle"* and also impossible for a rich man to enter the Kingdom of God if his riches come first. The Eye of a Needle was actually a single gate in the wall surrounding Jerusalem that was notorious for allowing a man to go through but his camel could not follow. If you were a visitor to the wall and didn't know about that gateway, you were tricked.

"Okay, stick out your tongue." (Isaiah 57:4) How many times does a doctor say that in a day? In its original form in the Scripture, it refers to a gesture of defiance. God is speaking to those who are transgressors who are full of falsehoods. So, be careful the next time you open your mouth wide and stick out your tongue to make a statement. Children stick out their tongues at each other and adults flippantly show their tongue. They certainly did it in Old Testament days. That Scripture is 2700 years old.

"I'm so sure about this, I will never flinch. My face is set like a flint." (Isaiah 50:7) Isaiah is stating that he has made up his mind for God and His glory and nothing will change it, no matter the smiter, the spitter, the shamer, or the condemner *(vs. 6-9)*.

"Aha!" (Isaiah 44:16) I've found it or we've made a discov-

ery or we have felt something that is very satisfying. The Scripture indicates that very thing. A man set a fire and warmed himself in front of it and, it felt so good to the body, he said, *"A-H-A!"*

"That is good for nothin'!" (Isaiah 44:10) God declares that if you form a god or mold an image, it is profitable (good) for nothing.

"You'd better set your house in order." (Isaiah 38:1) The Lord is telling king Hezekiah who was seriously sick, through His prophet Isaiah, to get his house in order. In other words, *"Get your affairs in order and prepare for tough times."*

"Here a little and there a little." (Isaiah 28:10) Literally, it means what it says. Do whatever you do, incrementally, step by step. To teach the children of Israel, God applied this method of "little by little" to increase their understanding of His ways and wishes, so they wouldn't be "childish" as His chosen ones.

"That's good . . . nail it down." (Isaiah 22:23) That is exactly what God did. He took the "house of David" and fastened it as a nail to a sure place for a glorious throne in the history of His people.

"He was without a stitch of clothes. He was naked and barefoot." (Isaiah 20:2) You aren't naked without taking your shoes off. The Lord asked Isaiah to visit Egypt and Ethiopia for three years to get their attention when the prophet

spoke His word in foreign lands. It was God's way to warn of their pending captivity by the king of Assyria in which they would be stripped. The Lord wanted the Egyptians and Ethiopians to flee to His protection and care.

"Don't peep a word of this"or "Don't make a peep." (Isaiah 10:14) God is prophesying in which there will be a time when He will gather the whole earth together and, with amazement, they won't utter a word or make a peep of a sound.

"That smells. . . it stinks!" (Isaiah 3.24) God said it Himself. He was upset with the "daughters of Zion" who were haughty and stiff necked *(vs. 16-26)*. When God speaks we should listen.

"From the soul of your foot to the crown of your head." (Isaiah 1:6, 3:17) God used this expression to indicate what happens will involve the whole body, from top to bottom or bottom to top.

"Come on, let's reason together" or "Let's talk it over." (Isaiah 1:18) God actually said it to address His interest in mankind to come to Him, Who is so reasonable, He is righteous about it. He would take your red sins and make them white like wool.

"You know, the little foxes spoil the vine." (Song of Solomon 2:15) Solomon was the first to say it in his book. It is absolutely true. The wisest of all in his day has an outstanding

proverb here. Jesus repeated it in the New Testament.

"I am love-sick." (Song of Solomon 5:8) This is Solomon's unrequited love's desire to find him for herself. She (the Shulamite woman) put all the daughters of Jerusalem on notice that if they see Solomon to let him know that she is passionately looking for him as her beloved.

"Two heads are better than one." (Ecclesiastes 4:9) That is the book with so many basic concepts that we refer to today. If we put our heads together we can be more productive with our labor. That is the same book where we get the expression, *"There is nothing new under the sun."*

"There is nothing like a nagging woman." (Proverbs 27:15) A steady drip on a very rainy day and a nagging woman are similar. *Proverbs 21:9 &19* says that it is better to live in the corner of a the housetop or in the attic than to live with a brawling (nagging) woman in a big house. *Verse 19* says it's better to live in the wilderness than with that woman.

Generations have come and gone and the words have affected their lives by the contents between the covers of the Bible from beginning to end. These words and thoughts have filtered into our everyday chatter and influence us daily.

That's where all that stuff comes from, the Word of God. God even gave us a lifetime of words and many don't even know where they come from, but there it is, the Bible.

23

You Can Be Old and Still Minister

I wrote once about a friend of mine, 'a spiritual confidant', named Sister Fuller. Quite a bit transpired in her life over the past few years. Her husband became quite ill and had to go into a nursing home. Some of this happened about the time Hurricane Rita hit Texas.

Sister Fuller was moved to a residence adjoining the nursing facility where he had been taken. She would walk back and forth for breakfast, lunch and supper at the age of 82 and visit with him. He was incapacitated for a time, but the two kept close. If she is still alive and on this earth, she is in her nineties.

Brother Fuller was able to stabilize and recover enough from his illness that he could get around better. He would go and witness and share with the other residents of the nursing facility. He was ecstatic that he was reaching some of the others who lived there as an ambassador for the Gospel.

Sister Fuller stayed close by and then finally he succumbed to his illness. She continued to go back and forth and carry on her husband's work to minister to the needs of the elderly who lived there.

As I told you before, she has been a woman who was always there for me. She comforted me through the divorce with my children's dad and several years of heartache. She had been diligent in praying for my children, especially my youngest daughter. Her heart was very touched by the mere thought of Cristi and how sweet her heart was. She never met my daughter, Cristi, but there was connection there that I just cannot explain.

There may be someone who is elderly, but they fit the description of this lady who has touched my life with her ability to listen and pray. She has touched Heaven for many a woman, young and old who needed her listening heart. Her words were always full of wisdom and understanding. They were always words I needed to hear at the time.

She always had a merry heart and so much compassion. She treated me as if I were one of her own children. The Bible says in *Proverbs 17:24* that *"A merry heart doeth good like a medicine and a broken spirit drieth the bones."* It certainly does.

God has planted different people in my path throughout my life and I have enjoyed the Edna Martins, Rozelia Morris' and the Sister Fullers that have whisked through my life leaving me with a sense of blessedness. My mom has been gone for over forty years and God has supplied me with people who have that same spirit of motherly kindness or just sisters, who were considerably older than I.

Now that I am seventy-two, I must make myself available to the younger women who need comfort in their hardships. Many churches don't have that anymore, but even my great grandmother was a prayer warrior before I was born.

Our lives don't lose their effectiveness, but they become more seasoned when our strength is founded in the Lord. We actually act out what we saw someone else do for us when we reach out to another. Christ in us wipes away the tears and heals our heart through the hands of others and hearts of others in our lives.

"Joy comes in the morning" and the vessel that brings it could be a young person, an elderly person, a minister or a woman cleaning the hospital room where you lie.

When my mother was in the hospital and they had diagnosed her with breast Cancer, there was a precious black woman who worked in housekeeping in the hospital. Her name was Anna Suggs. She and my mother shared what Christ had done for them and they prayed together.

My prayer for each of us who receives the joy of the presence of Christ is this, Lord walk with my feet, touch with my hands and hear the needs of others with my heart and just use me. There is a song called, *"Use Me."* I heard it after I had been praying for that same thing for years; *"Just use me, Lord."*

That's what Sister Fuller did and would still be doing if the Lord has not taken her home. If He has, I know she must be sitting at the feet of Jesus by her husband and they would have the sweetest smiles on their faces, because He is the one she talked about for so many years to so many people. Her faith would have come to be reality.

Psalm 37:25 says: "I have been young and now am old, but I have never seen the righteous forsaken, nor His seed begging bread."

As you leaf through the pages of the Bible, you will find that many were called in their middle to older years. The Bible also says—God's call is without repentance. If God called you at one time in your life, that call is still in effect until your life ceases, in my estimation.

Sister Fuller knew that she was called to minister to others. She never put down her phone or failed to answer when I needed her and now her little walker clicks to the beat of the same drummer. She took up the challenge in her eighties to spread the Gospel with a heart full of love for her Savior and her precious husband. Her mind is clear and her goal is certain. She has worked for the King of Kings and Lord of Lords and drawn in the net for those who commit to Christ. She is truly one of God's chosen.

She'll tell you that she's not too old to minister to others in need, especially those without the salvation we all so desperately need to carry us through. So, hats off to Sister Marcelyn Fuller. There will surely be a "Crown of Righteousness" she can place at the feet of Jesus Christ, our Savior.

Her living legacy to me is that I may step gracefully into my older years and anticipate even more usefulness. I love people and have ministered to quite a few over the years, but being seventy-two, I expect even more to cross my path. I am experiencing that and I'm so grateful for opportunities to be able to draw people into the walk they have always wanted. Many who walk in heartache want peace—only Jesus Christ can bring it.

Thank you Sister Fuller for being there through my tears, heartaches and laughter in the Lord. Thank you for your words from the Lord and your precious prayers.

24

A Man Delivered from Saul to Paul

In Acts 9, Saul was in full swing to indeed rid this world of Christians. In *Acts 9:1-6*, it says, *"And Saul, yet breathing out threatenings and slaughter against the disciples of the Lord, And desired of him letters to Damascus to the synagogues that if he found any of this way [the Way], whether they were men or women, he might bring them bound unto Jerusalem. And as he journeyed, he came near Damascus: and suddenly there shined round about him a light from heaven: And he fell to earth, and heard a voice saying unto him, Saul, Saul, why persecutest thou me? And he said, Who art thou, Lord? And the*

Lord said, "I am Jesus, whom thou persecutest, it is hard to kick against the pricks." And he trembling and astonished said, "Lord what wilt thou have me to do?" And the Lord said unto him, "Arise and it shall be told thee what thou must do." And, you know what follows, he got up from there blind.

As happens so often, we look at the externals of an individual and that's that. What Saul was doing was brutal and bloodthirsty, for sure. It took an encounter with Jesus Christ, Himself, to see his horrible mistake. This Saul was on a path with blinders due to radical religious zeal. But Christ, in a split second, changed the heart of Saul. There was an exchange of one blindness for another blindness until he could really see the "light." This blindness allowed the Christians to minister to Saul for the sake of the Church of the "Lord" Jesus Christ. Saul was now helplessly in the hands of those he religiously vowed to send to their deaths. Would they kill him before he could kill any more of them? The word was out in the Christian community that ol' Saul was the worst of the worst towards any of the followers of Christ. What the believers in Jesus showed Paul was LOVE, the singular trademark of the Christian Church! God had provided a chain of events to show soon-to-be Paul, no longer Saul, the Way. For three days he could not see and consumed no food. He was given a crash course in processing the information shown to him by Jesus on that road to Damascus.

Paul did great works for the Lord. Paul wrote he was leaving those things behind and looking to those things before to press toward the mark of the prize of the high calling of God in Christ Jesus. Up until then, he killed Christians with all his might. He was doing a whole-hearted devotion to his God. The instant encounter with Jesus immediately transformed the life of this man forever. He always remarked later that he counted all other things a loss (wasteless), for the excellency of the knowledge of Christ Jesus the Lord. For most Christians from then to the present, if asked what person in the New Testament would they want to most emulate, surely, it would be Paul. He gained everything but lost his life by the hand of a government in Rome with a beheading.

Originally, Paul was all in one way and then was all in another WAY. Don't give up on folks. No matter how poorly it looks in one direction, it can be turned around instantaneously and go in another direction directly 180 degrees to the opposite. Don't give up on your children and young people. No matter how far out there they go, they can turn around and come home. The Prodigal Son said, *"I must go back to my father."*

And as soon as he saw his father, he remarked, *"I have sinned."* There can be the regeneration of a generation—don't give up! Paul stated that of all sinners he was chief. If he is any indication, there is hope for every last lost soul. I mean, don't give up on anyone you are praying for, even for months and years. He doesn't give up, so why should we? It is God's will that none should perish.

Don't let it scare you. Paul's salvation experience scared many a Christian in the early days. In *Acts 9:13*, a believer named Ananias was told to go and pray for Saul's eyes to be opened. He did so reluctantly because he knew Saul's reputation. I'm sure he said to himself, *"Only God can help Saul."* Well, He did! When Ananias obeyed the Lord and prayed for him, it was as if scales fell from his eyes.

Immediately afterwards, He began to preach Jesus as the Son of God. Even Peter and disciples at Jerusalem were distant to Paul, at first. They found out first hand that Paul was now God's man and it invigorated them. *"If He can do it for Paul, He can do it for anybody!"* Because Paul was ordained to speak (for Jesus) salvation to the Gentiles, other than the Jews, God ordained him as the Thirteenth Apostle, amazingly 12 + 1.

I believe these are still New Testament times because we are still testifying to the new! Are you a Saul, awaiting the change? Has Jesus called your name and shown you that there must be a turnaround in your life? Our God is *"faithful and just to forgive,"* from the hard head to the tenderhearted—He loves you.

25

Are You Ready for the Battle?

A boxer has to train for the fight. He has to eat the right foods, watch what he drinks and build those muscles. A runner has to basically do the same thing or any athlete who wants to succeed. Each has to make a difference in their life styles and habits to set themselves apart for that superior physical edge. Football players have to have the right amount of sleep, an abundance of healthy foods. They are all looking to be championship caliber.

What would a soldier do to prepare for battle? You would think first and foremost that person would have to be in incredible physical condition, if it was the usual soldier, of course. But, for the battle to which I refer, the physical falls far behind in the ranking. My analogy doesn't hold up very long or does it? I'm talking about being in shape, however, least of all, the physical. My context is spiritual warfare, which requires as much commitment to the project as the top-notch athlete.

It has been said, *"If you don't deal with spirits, they won't deal with you. Leave them alone and they'll leave you alone."* Not so. We live in a spiritual world as much as a physical world.

The Bible will help us "shape up." *Ephesians 6:10* tells us, *"Finally, my brethren, be strong in the Lord, and in the power of His might."* How we are strong, in the spiritual sense, is by feeding our spirits with the right things. Man's spirit can be filled with the goodness of God; that rules out any junk. Without an infilling of the soul with the powerful teachings of Christ, the spirit man weakens, eventually with a total loss of vitality. You've heard the expression, *"I'm just a shell of a man."* When there is no "fill-up" of the graciousness of God, there is only a "ticker with no vigor." When you get run down, a "tune-up" won't even do the job. So, find your strength in the Lord—that's where the "power" is.

The Bible continues in *Ephesians 6:11 and 12, "Put on the whole armor of God, that ye may be able to stand against the wiles of the devil. For we wrestle not against flesh and blood, but against principalities, against powers, against the rulers of the darkness of this world, against spiritual wickedness in high places."*

Here the Word tells us that His strength includes a shielding against the adverse spirits at work in this world. I'll tell you some of what prompted this subject. There is a sensing all around me that we may be drawing to the end of the age, the sense that something cataclysmic is near at hand. That something far greater than floods, earthquakes, tornadoes and hurricanes is about to occur. This is from people who are not "churchy." They never darken the doors of a church. Their exercise is to brace themselves for a forceful, foreboding event they can't put into words. Well, the Word tells us the negative forces at work are the principal powers that rule darkness in this world, against spirit wickedness.. You can be protected by God's Armor, also spiritual and enduring, put on in faith.

There are TV shows dealing with this subject on many channels . . . ghosts, spirits, mysticism, the supernatural, the paranormal, the metaphysical. You have shows saying you can deal with darkness in your own power. "You've got the poww-err."

I stand on God's Holy Word to tell you that the only overcoming power is given to us by Jesus Christ who said, *"Whatsoever you shall bind on Earth shall be bound in Heaven, and whatsoever you shall loose on earth shall be loosed in heaven."* God has given us the authority to speak to these invisible enemies and they have to flee. There are those who have troubled sleep, with dreams that literally torment them. Speak to your night in the Name of Jesus before you retire.

We have all authority over our situations, if we have asked Jesus into our hearts. If you don't have Jesus as your Savior and Lord, ask Jesus into your heart and be saved and all this power is yours.

There are those who are always uptight during their waking hours. When you awaken, speak to your day in the Name of Jesus. We can speak with His authority that He has vested in us through His Word and He will do the rest. One of the reputations Jesus received early on in His ministry while here on earth was, *"Who is this man that even the winds and the waves obey him? Never a man spake as this man!"*

Now, I'm not attempting to make anyone into a grotesquely super-being like "Ironman" or "Captain America" but let's become VICTORS and not the victims. Don't expect to be coddled, cuddled or cradled through this life. Be the CONQUEROR that God through Jesus Christ intends you to be. Be an OVERCOMER and have control over the outcome of your life. Straighten up and stand for something and stick it out through thick and thin. You don't have to be a wimp in the Kingdom of God. Stiffen that spine and stop that whine. Be a spiritual warrior who fights the good fight of faith. John said in *St. John's Gospel*, the first chapter, *"He [Jesus] came unto His own [the Jews] and they received Him not. But to as many as received Him [into their heart], to them gave He the P-O-W-E-R to become the sons of God, even to as many as believe on His Name..."*

26

Are You Ready?

Have You Prepared Yourself?

There are things going on around us that seem to be

weighing our minds down. As I look around, there is a Scripture that my continuing articles are based on. *Revelations 12:11* says this, *"And they overcame him [Satan] by the blood of the Lamb, and by the word of their testimony; and they loved not their lives unto the death."* They overcame Satan by the blood of the Lamb and testifying about the things God has done for them and the storms He has brought them through. Here are some testimonies.

I met a young woman some years ago in Texas. She went to a large metropolitan mainstream church. She stood out in a crowd, especially in the choir on Sunday mornings. After a few weeks, I got to know her. I went to some of the ladies' meetings and had the honor of meeting her. She was a born-again Muslim. She was so excited about the love of the Lord that she could not get enough of the music and the praise and preaching of God's Word. She had the freedom of being a woman in America.

In talking to her, she told me she had married an American man and when she found the Lord, her family disowned her and threatened to kill her. In spite of all that, her spirit was exalted in the Lord and she was excited about life in which there was no bondage because of the joy of the Lord.

Then I heard about a man at a revival, a huge historic revival in this century. He had walked round and round the building where it was commencing and he was trying to find someone to talk to about this Jesus from this dynamic

100

ministry. The minister led him to the Lord that day and afterward he said, *"Yes, I have found this Jesus. I have peace."*

Also, there was a young man whose family practiced their religions and his question to my friend on the internet was this, *"Why is there so much hatred and killing?"* My friend told him there doesn't have to be. She told him about Jesus and he received Christ into His heart over the internet and it relieved all his worry about hatred. There are others who have come to the Lord through his transformation and testimony.

I personally know a few who have come to the Lord out of witchcraft, which is like going from the dark to the light! One woman who came to a Bible study back in Texas had been doing her incantations and the table caught on fire where she was practicing her craft. Everything on the table burned except her Bible. That was the only thing spared and she realized that she had been following the wrong master.

There are seven things that God hates. *Proverbs 6:16* says this, *"These six things doth the Lord hate, yea, seven are an abomination unto Him. A proud look, a lying tongue, and hands that shed innocent blood. A heart that deviseth wicked imaginations, feet that be swift in running to mischief. A false witness, and he that soweth discord among brethren."*

I want to point out that God hates these sins; all sin is an abomination to Him. The Bible indicates that sinfulness is a stench to His nostrils.

It is not an easy thing to love the sinner and hate the sin, but that's what God does. He loves all His children. They all come from "Father Abraham." He has a way out for everyone. He desires that none should perish, but have everlasting life through Jesus Christ, His Son. That is why God sent His only begotten into this world to be the ultimate sacrifice for our sin. *John 3:16* is the Scripture many of us were taught from our infancy to adulthood. There are so many still who have yet to hear the Name of Jesus and realize there is peace in that Name, peace that calms the storms.

It seems too easy to accept Christ and be made free of such things that cause us to transgress, but it is actual and effectual. Christ is the answer to any and all problems. The Martyrs, who *"loved not their lives unto the death"* but loved the Lord, would tell you: to live for Christ is the utmost goal with amazing results! Many would call these fanatics, Jesus freaks, but those who laid down their lives stood for what was at stake and gave us testimony for our sake.

For all the hatred and blood-letting there is in this world, there is that much more love in Christ Jesus. He died to save, heal and deliver and I am so grateful to know the Son of the Most High God. I am not alone, nor forsaken, or rejected, but merely forgiven.

I know His return is soon! We are experiencing those wars

and rumors of wars Jesus spoke about. Israel is on high alert while I write and you read! He's coming. Be ready. Are you? Ready, that is.

27

Being in the Dark

Have you ever walked into a dark building out of the sunlight and it took your eyes a little bit to recover from the light to the darkness? I have. Especially when you go to a movie. You go in and have a difficult time seeing a seat. Or, vise versa, you exit the theatre and have an awkward time readjusting to the sunlight. Have you ever had that happen in life? I have. It has been said out of my mouth for years, *"I find myself in the dark in broad daylight, sometimes!"*

When you are going through a trial it is as if you walk into the dark and can't find your way around. It is as if you are walking on the edge and have to feel your way around to keep from falling or to get your bearings. Oh, you and I hear it all the time. *"I see the light at the end of the tunnel."* Oh yea? Sometimes, I've been in a tunnel with NO light at the other end.

You can be walking through the park or down a path and think someone is following you and panic. There are any number of scenarios that can cause us to loose sight and other senses and there goes our composure in the dark where there is little light. Often, when I see a blind person, they are tapping around with a long, thin white stick with a red tip for careful direction. I know of a bigger stick that gives me direction when I feel blinded by immediate circumstances and it is found in the *23rd Psalm: "Though I walk through the valley of the shadow . . . , I will fear no evil: for Thou art with me; Thy ROD and Thy STAFF they comfort me . . . "* It has come to my attention that someone who has lost their physical sight has enhanced other senses to compensate for their loss.

Thus, I've come to my "senses" and learned to be calm... there has to be an answer. I can usually figure it out and the solution is simple: find the switch and turn on the light! When you surround the situation with nearly blinding light, it is not a conundrum anymore. Now, just because I've found my "little light" doesn't mean that I have enough light to light the world. The world has some dark, dark problems. At least, It is nice to think I have some glow to my life. Take for example, the lightning bug. It is easy to see one in the darkness; quite a contrast. But, overall not much Illumination. If you collect a canning jar full of lightning bugs it is like a light bulb and you can light up a pup tent. Therefore, Jesus' order of the day is incredibly apropos: *"Let your light so shine before men..."*

Verily, verily, I am not being simplistic. The problems of

this world have darkened us globally. If I watch too much news on TV, there is a gloomy cloud that seems to hang over me. I know I'm getting older (hopefully, a little wiser) so I have a period of reference that spans over six decades. This doesn't seem like the same old world our parents raised us in. As I get older, I wish to get lighter and lighter. I would like it said of me, *"Go to Collene. She can shed more light on the subject."*

It's like we are one filament bulbs glowing dimly when we don't have the power of Christ in our lives. When we let Christ in, (Who stands at every heart's door knocking for entrance), we increase our filament power many times over. It doesn't take Watson, I assume, to realize "higher power" brings greater light! We go from under-lit to ultra-bright.

When we walk in the dark in the physical and spiritual sense, it may be an illness of a close friend or family member, a divorce or financial problems; or it could be depression that one just cannot throw off. These are all examples of *"the valley of the shadow of death"*.

What we need to cling to when the shadows come are God's promises. *Hebrews 3:5b* says, *"for He hath said, I will never leave thee, nor forsake thee."* What a comfort in any circumstance when you are going through something that overshadows every part of your mind, soul and spirit. Take heed when you are going through that dry, dark place. *Psalms 121:2, "My help cometh from the Lord, which made heaven and earth."* Walking in darkness, physical or spiritual, is troubling to our comfort zone and throws us off balance. We are not at ease and anxiety wants to set in. This particular Scripture helped my mother through the valley of Cancer.

Get control of this counter-productivity. Jesus said, *"I am the light of the world. I am the light that lighteth every man."* Throw the switch! Light up your life. When others see the light, they are drawn to it in the dark. God's element is more filament power. LIGHT is an area of expertise that only the Lord has mastered, for He is the Master.

Be sharp as a tack and poke holes in the darkness of this world and let His light shine through.

28

Chasing Crows

How did the battle begin and when did this life start into a lifetime of drinking and spiraling downward? The following poem is the testimony of a man named Crow. Crow goes to church with us and a man wrote this poem for him and maybe it will explain how his struggle began. Your suspicion is correct: Crow has an American Indian heritage.

Chasing Crows
by Dennis Colcek

Hush little baby, some whiskey rubbed on my gums.
Becoming an alcoholic,
while my mother rocks and hums.
Put a little more in a bottle,
tainted milk will help him sleep.
A pathway to destruction, I didn't run, I took a leap.
Attention wasn't easy, youngest of nine, I held it dear,
Abandonment was the issue, loneliness is now the fear;
Drinking and drugs became a lifestyle,
a broken marriage it produced.
A lifetime of deception,
a broken heart that became seduced.
Living in my prison that was far beyond my mind;
Shadows all around me, a real life I left behind.
Dreams are all but whispers, and freedom's all but dead;
Death's door is all but waiting, down to darkness I was led.
Body art became my image, as for me there were no rules;
This life it needed fixing, but I didn't have the tools.
Rehab became my home, full of trembles and the shakes.
"God just take my life, no matter what it takes."
Passing blood became so common,
this body torn through the years.
My gun was loaded. I was ready, take me from these tears.
An awakening was coming; there was a calling for this life.
I needed surgery on my spirit,
and the Lord had brought His knife.

He took a broken man, and now a mission this life holds.
By His awesome power, He took my past,
and broke the molds.
For years, I chased these crows
from trying to steal this seed,
But God, through His love, at last this man has been freed.

As you can gather from this, Crow was introduced to the taste for alcohol at an early age, even as his mother rocked him in her arms. The taste and the affect of alcohol took root in his life as an infant. It was easy for his mother, with nine children, to take the easy way out, to soothe the gums. The influence could be the father, as well. One man told me that he felt like he would be a man when he could crush a beer can in his hand like his dad. That was the image of the man he wanted to be.

Mama introduced him to the taste of alcohol and it accelerated from there. As with many others, he had no answers to the problems. He was the product of the fruit of someone giving an alien substance to a child. The thought was that this is okay, never realizing the deep roots that twist into the character of one's mind and soul. It became a struggle, a battle if you will, to fit into the norm. The only way to overcome these demonic strongholds is by the blood of Jesus Christ. The Lord brought him the help he needed. Crow has chased "crows" away from childhood upwards and then the crow that would have stolen the seed of the Gospel chased him until about seven years ago when he gave his heart to Jesus.

Crow is still learning. God is revealing Himself to him each and every day. Christ is stepping in daily in this brother's behalf to make a better way for him.

II Corinthians 10:4-5 describes the battle that Crow and many others face, *"For though we walk in the flesh, we do not war after the flesh. (For the weapons of our warfare are not carnal, but mighty through the pulling down of strongholds.) Casting down imaginations, and every high thing that exalteth itself against the knowledge of God, and bringing into captivity every thought to the obedience of Christ: . . ."*

What may start seemingly innocent can usher in our destruction at the earliest of ages. Our memories lie full of scars. These scars are baggage that act as weights on our back which can be mightily lifted by the Lord, Who even heals scars.

With each healing, comes more victory over those deeds planted so long ago. Those memories that hold us back and defeat us have become our giants to be overcome through the blood of the Lamb. Crow spent most of his life learning this, but, in seven years, his Heavenly Father has taught him well. He knows that God is on His side.

Crow had nothing to crow about for many years, but now can shout it out: *"Jesus rescues and repairs!"* He has found peace. He is determined to finish the race. He has been set free by the blood of Jesus Christ. He has walked through *the valley of the shadow of death* and now *walks in newness of life. John 8:36* says, *"If the Son therefore shall make you free, you shall be free indeed."*

Crow passed into glory several years ago. The most I knew about him, at the time, was that he was in every service and he was very quiet. He loved the Lord and made himself available to do what God wanted him to do. He's flying high now.

29

Christ is the Only Hope that Brings Us Change

Christ has made a change in multitudes of lives! He made a change in my life and that change began about 64 years ago. He has given me change with an eternal hope. We hear these words concerning life - change is constant and hope is hard to find. My personal testimony is that with His transforming power, the change is concrete and a sense of hope is complete. So, as our surroundings change, as they certainly will, there is the constancy of permanent, personal changelessness!

When the man lay at the Pool of Bethesda, unable to mobilize himself, Jesus told him, *"Be thou made whole."* Change came and hope was restored. He had lain by that pool for years helplessly, when Jesus passed by with a WORD.

When the woman touched the hem of Jesus' garment, she was healed of an issue of blood after many years of suffering. A truly remarkable difference came.

The ten lepers were healed.

Five thousand were fed by the Master from a basket filled with five loaves of bread and two fish.

Jesus is the marvelous Maker of things and the Re-maker of lives. I am always, unceasingly amazed at how He makes the impossible possible. He moves the unmovable, thinks the unthinkable and creates the inconceivable! Jesus said *that all things are possible to him that believes.* You want some change in your life, Jesus can give you some?! You want hope against all hope, Jesus can give you some?! I heard a saying recently that states: If you don't like the way you were born, try being "born again."

Here's power. There was a man named Crossy Malone and several of our church members back in Texas went to visit him right after services. We would sing and minister to him through prayer and Scripture. He had stomach cancer and his wife Teresa told us that she believed that because of those visits and all that prayer, he never had one pain during that horrible illness. He passed away, but the Lord brought comfort to Crossy in the midst of his darkest hours.

When I accepted the Lord as a child, I had no idea the difference the Lord would make in my life. I knew that He was important to me and in accepting Him, I would have His hand on me. Through the years, He has given me strength to stand and to withstand the storms of life that have blown my way. He opened my eyes and lifted forever the veil of tears.

Christ has made a difference in so many lives. There is one man we met a couple of years ago, whom we will call "Rangle," in whom the Lord has turned around by 180 degrees and is now His servant. The change the Lord has made in him from being a roustabout is making changes in others, as he shares his testimony. The Lord is beginning to restore what the rancid odor of sin had destroyed in his life. His relationship with his wife is being restored. He has begun to have a relationship with his sons and grandchildren. The Lord is using him in the ministry—how marvelous. I know story after story of helpless lives that have been hopefully changed. There is only one initiator of personal renovation through regeneration—that's Jesus.

Many people have an idea of what they could be, but somehow cannot achieve it. With the help of the Lord, that goal can be met. Sometimes we have to ask the Lord to help us to see ourselves as He sees us. We are hopelessly lost and undone without God's only Son; Jesus is the Hope of Glory and His Heavenly Father sent Him to be the answer to each and every problem in our lives. Wouldn't it be wonderful to wake up every morning asking the Lord Jesus Christ as to what you can accomplish together in each new day?

Psalms 145:18 says, *"The Lord is nigh unto all that call upon Him, to all that call upon Him in truth. He will fulfill the desire of them that fear Him: He also will hear their cry, and will save them."*

Remember Job and all that he went through. At the end of his testing, he had more than at the beginning. He had lost it all due to the trials and because of his faith and trust in God, he received restoration of far more than he had lost.

No obstacle is so big that Christ cannot intervene. If you want a better life, a brighter life, a blessed life, find the Lord personally in your life. If I could, I would "rope" you in with hope. If I could, I would "hang" the change over your head. I can't do any of that for you. That's why I say you need to do it personally for yourself. Nobody, I mean, nobody, can do it for you. But, if you want it, it's available. He is near at hand. He's waiting and ready. Jesus is "Hope and Change" . . . . .

30

Christmas, a Time of Hopefulness

Is Christmas time a season of hopeful reminiscence or another period of loneliness for you? It is a celebration of a birthday that should make us jubilant of the God-man Who gave us hope? His objective was to give to all an opportunity to eternal life. While Christmas generally gives us a warm feeling inside, we must remember that there are always some who are suffering from the memories of losses at this time of year, some to a heart wrenching degree. And as the most giving people in the world, Americans will valiantly try to do their part this year also.

I feel like the most prominent thing to speak for this Christmas are promises. *Psalms* was King David's high point. This book of the Bible speaks many promises and for those individuals who have ever experienced the truth of the Word of God, those words of hope have been esteemed valuable.

For example, in *Psalms 37:25* David says, *"I was once young but now I am old, and I have never seen the righteous forsaken, nor his seed begging for bread."*

As I walk through the recesses of my mind, I remember my special Christmases with my Mom and Dad. We didn't have much but we had each other and that was enough. We didn't have a lot of privileges but we possessed the blessings of comfort and security. My parents and much older brothers had everything set up for me to make sure I had my heart's desire. My Dad had serious illnesses and my Mom struggled until she became sick with breast Cancer. Nonetheless, there was always enough. We appreciated everything that was under the tree. What I remember most was our rich relationship with each other and the rich relationship we had with the Lord. Our Lord in the Old Testament was called, *"El Shaddai,"* which means, the God Who is always enough to meet your needs. Christmas, through my parents, taught me that there was always something there when something was needed. The tree was adorned with ornaments; however, our household was adorned with love. I tried to share that spirit with my three children when they were growing up those many years ago.

After those warm words, let us talk about the other side of the coin. For those who are at comfort and at ease, there are thousands more who are in the midst of trying times and, maybe, gift-giving "dry" times. During this time, think of Christmases past and the possibility of Christmases future. You probably did not light into this plight on your own. Christmas can still provide warmth if you put your heart into it. The gifts are not everything. Really, your setback is a setup for God to do the miraculous in your life. Remember, the Gift that God gave when He gave us His Son, the greatest gift of all. There is a song that says,

"If it gets down to it, take this world and give me Jesus." I literally can't stand it when anyone wants to take Christ out of Christmas by X'ing Him out. It disturbs me to no end. There is no such thing as "X-mas"!

I pray all who read this will recognize that the Christ has brought you this far. I don't know how much you have or if everything is running smoothly in your life. I only know that when the rough times have come to me, that little baby in that manger, whose birthday we celebrate, grew to be the King of Kings and Lord of Lords. He went from the cradle to Kingship. He went from the manger to the management of the Universe!

I know it appears to be out-of-place to try to be "warm and fuzzy" about Christmas and still deal with the unseemly side of the street. I guess I'm encouraging you to be sure you give more than you get for this season. It is the way God is. It is the way He wants us to be. The Bible says, *"Give and it shall be given to you, good measure, pressed down, shaken together and running over shall be added to your bosom". Luke 6:38.* Just as Christ gave His life for us, there are some around the world who believe so strongly in Him that they will give there lives for Him.

When you see a soldier coming home, GIVE the meet and greet. When you see the Cookeville Rescue Mission bell ringers and buckets, or the block parties for the Bread of Life Rescue Mission, GIVE.

Baby Jesus wasn't just any baby, He was the "Hope of Glory". He is the Son of the Most High God. That's why He gives us the highest of hope. So, as much as there is hustle and bustle and gloss and glitter for the end of the year, put in perspective that the GIFT has already been given. Hold on to that gift because if you never get another gift in another Christmas, you have been "given" because you are "forgiven".

Christ went from the cradle to the cross to give you sufficiency. *"He will supply all your needs according to His riches in glory."* A song we sing often in church: *"From heaven to earth, from the earth to the cross, from the cross to the grave, from the grave to the sky, Lord, we lift your name on high."*

Enthusiastically, my husband, Kent and I pray you have a most favorable Christmas and that all is well in your home with your family. Make your special guest within your family circle J-E-S-U-S.

31

Day by Day Struggles

Day by day, we face struggles some are new and some are old. Some are brand new experiences and others are nothing new at all. Some of the things we face are similar to others with a different name and different smell. It's as if the first time wasn't enough. The same type of thing has to come after us again. Some have been married several times and others have stayed married for years.

We don't always realize we are having a struggle until it is upon us and we are in a raging battle. It is almost as if we are stepping into a pool of quick sand. We begin to try to get loose and find ourselves being sucked in deeper and deeper. Before we know it, we are up to our necks.

The devil is that way, he makes his move in such a way that we don't even know he is there. He makes it a subtle approach, maybe a whisper or a whim that we think is our own idea and it comes from what we think is virtually from nowhere. Not all ideas are from nowhere. To be point blank—all ideas are from somewhere.

Each one of you has a testimony that would put the enemy, Satan, to flight. You survived something that was meant to destroy your life, your very existence, You may have been a Tim Tebow who was not meant to survive from the very beginning and the Lord had His hand on you to see to it you were born in spite of perilous circumstances. You may not have seen your purpose yet.

My mother thought I was a tumor and the doctor told her, *"No ma'am, that's no tumor, it's a little baby. That little tumor has a head, two little arms and two little legs."* My mom also thought she would never have a baby girl because she had already lost two baby girls.

Your life meant something special to your mom and dad and to the Lord, Himself. You may not even know how special you are to the Lord, but you are here. You are a walking blessing, if not then—you can be. You have made it this far with each breath you take, each step you take. Some people say they know they're alive because they read the obituaries and see their name is not there, with a bit of a chuckle.

My first high school reunion was a shocker for me because the Vietnam war had taken so many of my classmates. I graduated in 1963 and there was a long list of names that had suffered loss from that war and several unexpected deaths. I don't mind telling you that God has had His hand on my life several times I can tell you of and He probably spared me some times I didn't even know about.

My husband can tell you about Vietnam. He went into the service as a conscientious objector and never carried a weapon. He let his grades get down a little in college and they drafted him. He was studying at Gulf Coast Bible College in Houston. No, we didn't meet then, but we could have. That's another story. But he went into the army and was a medic. He served the men he marched beside. He saw more bloodshed in two years than you or I have seen in a lifetime.

That kind of warfare is another thing that slips up on you.

Those boys that went over to fight in Vietnam got on the backside too. Kent, as many others, has faced the harrows of Agent Orange. About forty percent of those men are still living and around 60 percent have succumbed to the after effects. If you ever see Kent, you can ask him and he will tell you he would do it all again for the freedom of our country, not because he enjoyed it, but because he loves our country and our freedom.

Just a few weeks ago, he was finally able to watch the movie, *"Hacksaw Ridge"* and I looked over at Kent and he was crying uncontrollably. Something that had been said by Desmond Doss triggered a memory and God healed something in Kent's mind from Vietnam and the war.

There is help with all these daily battles, spiritual, physical and mental. That help comes from the Lord. *(Psalms 121 and Ephesians 6)*

Remember there is power in the tongue and you have the ability to resist the devil and he will flee. My son learned that about those shadows and creepy crawly things on the wall at night when he was about ten. He was always scared at night and would call me to come to him and I finally told him he didn't have to be afraid and that fear was the opposite of faith. I prayed with him and told him he could take authority over those shadows on the wall or what his little mind could scare him with and he listened. He learned that Jesus was his best friend and could help him to sleep at night without being afraid.

The same Jesus that helped you as a child to not be afraid is able to help you daily and does. There are those of you who have not yet figured what your purpose is, but the Lord is still revealing Himself to you in ways that make you just shake your head in unbelief. It is true the Lord loves you so much that it is hard to believe, but He is there with open arms and the least of your worries concern Him as much as the big ones do.

Exodus 14:14 says, "You hold your peace and I will fight for you."

32

Daylight and Dark

We all hear about the deeds done in the dark. What I mean is, the deeds from the darker side of humanity. We are learning constantly about child abuse and spousal abuse. It is dauntlessly done daily within the four corners of this country. This news could cause the most toughened heart to tremble and quake. Evil truly walks among us and makes a mockery of the gift of life that God has given us.

There was a particular day that my daughter called me and

told me she had rolled her truck three times, around 1 PM and had survived without a scratch. I had a song of praise on my lips all morning long at work. I didn't say anything to my customers about what I was carrying in my heart, but when I was waiting for a customer or straightening shelves, I was singing, *"Lord, You are the air I breathe, You are the air I breathe, Your holy presence living in me."* Over and over, for at least four hours, it ruminated in my mind. It began when I walked through the door to the store that day. (Who says you can't live for the Lord and make a living at the same time? I was dwelling on the goodness of the Lord and being good to my customers, simultaneously! And, I'm not really a multi-tasker.) Remember that thing about walking and chewing gum, that's me, but I guess I can when God is in it.

How about the little boy in Alabama? Someone told me there was a little boy who had been found in an ice chest after some horrific tornadoes. They had searched for the child frantically for days and finally found him without a hair on his head harmed. They asked how he had known to get into the chest and the three year old said that a man with wings told him to get into the cooler and he would be safe. No, I didn't talk to eyewitnesses, but a friend in whom I have confidence told me what he knew.

So, what I am saying with these short stories is that sure there is a lot of darkness out there. But, for every advance of darkness there is an abundance of light. I truly believe that we are living in a day that God is still busy taking care of people, turning souls from gloom and doom to immortal illumination!

Oh, you say to yourself, that girl has some kind of a film over her eyes and she is not seeing clearly. People have made the comment, *"How can you believe all that?"* I suppose I'm a little like Paul the Apostle.

When the Lord Jesus knocked him off his donkey when traveling on the road to Damascus, he was temporarily blinded, as if scales over his eyes. But, a few days later, when his eyes were opened, he "saw the light," like that Hank Williams, Sr. song, *"I saw the light, I saw the light. No more in darkness, no more in night. Now, I'm so happy, no sorrow in sight. Praise the Lord, I saw the light!"* Please, forgive me for comparing myself to Saint Paul, but our experiences do have some similarities. St. Paul never looked back and neither do I.

So, for every strand of darkness around us, I see a "double portion of light." I see God making a difference in the hearts of people and giving them something to hold on to and helping them to make it through the "night" of day. JESUS IS THE LIGHT. He has brought lives to life and light from the midst of deadly, dark situations.

I know a married couple who were brought out of drugs and a lifestyle that was depressing to them and displeasing to God. I heard their testimony in person quite recently. The Lord has turned their lives around and given them land and a new home and all the amenities associated with it. Why this is so remarkable is that the Devil had stolen from them everything they owned, even their self-respect and the respect of their children.

1 Peter 2:9-10 applies to their lives and the lives of many others: *"But ye are a chosen generation, a royal priesthood, an holy nation, a peculiar people; that ye should show forth the praises of Him who hath called you out of darkness into his marvelous light: Which in time past were not a people, but are now the people of God: which had not obtained mercy, but now have obtained mercy."*

I love my life in the Lord and He gives me the light of His presence to clear my way through this dark world. It's like trekking through the wilderness at times, searching for the right path. God is a lover of souls and a giver of light. Did you know that when we get to Heaven, there is no switch to turn the lights out?! Jesus, Who is the Light here in these last days, will be the one and only ever-abiding Light in Heaven. It will be one eternal day. He is the difference in daylight and dark.

33

Encourage Yourself

This may seem all about me, but it is something that might help you in whatever your situation. When I worked at Walmart and Kent was so sick, I had a notebook of Scripture that would encourage me. I sang songs or hummed them to myself, praise songs that would pump me up to face the time at hand. The Bible tells us to encourage ourselves.

Some of you may remember the time my daughter flipped her truck three times on the way home from town and without a scratch on her. The truck was totalled, but she was in good shape except for being shaken up. All morning that morning I had been singing *"You are the air I breathe, Your Holy Word living in me."* I had heard nothing at that time. About 1 p.m., my oldest daughter called me and told me what had happened. You can't tell me that God didn't intervene because this mama's spirit was staying in the presence of the Lord while being busy about my work. He had stepped in and taken care of my child.

That time it was song; but most of the time for a season, my little notebook kept me going on my breaks. Such Scriptures as *Psalms 41:1-3* held me together better than duck tape. *"Blessed is he that considereth the poor: the Lord will deliver him in time of trouble. The Lord will preserve him, and keep him alive: and he shall be blessed upon the earth, and thou wilt not deliver him unto the will of the enemies. The Lord will strengthen him upon the bed of languishing: thou wilt make all his bed in his sickness."*

I wrote them down and then put them on the tables of my heart. I learned to lean on praise and the Word years ago. With all that we face today, whether it is the sickness of a loved one or financial problems, either or both are weapons of warfare in time of trouble. God's Words are like silver and gold when troubles come.

Things that are seemingly impossible need an application of *"Hear my cry, O God; attend unto my prayer. From the end of the earth will I cry unto thee when my heart is overwhelmed; lead me to the Rock that is higher than I." Psalms 68:1-3* addresses the problem of enemies. David said to drive his enemies away as smoke, but let the righteous be glad and rejoice greatly.

To some of you, your situation may seem so huge that you just cannot do such a simple thing as trust the God of all the universe who you cannot see; but when nothing else helps, how can you not just try it. You might like it. There are people all around us who are walking testimonies of the power of the living God. Christ is the same yesterday, today and forever. His Word is as powerful as it was when the Father spoke this world into existence.

126

I found years ago that praying Scripture works. It works when you are praying for your husband, to heal yourself and your marriage, your kids, your work situation, your parents. God moves when you give His Word back to Him. He hastens to perform it as it is written in Jeremiah. He knows your heart to start with, but when you begin to speak the Word, His Word back to Him, He knows you are catching on. You are proving to Him that your trust lies in Him. In *Isaiah*, the Word says that His Word will not come back void.

I lean on Him and God does not disappoint me. Sometimes things may not go exactly as I think they ought to. He is an awesome God who is not some god made out of clay or wood. He is not merely a man put on a pedestal. God is the unseen hand that leads and guides us to victory in our lives. Our Heavenly Father sent His Only Begotten Son to live the example before us and to die to set us free from all unrighteousness. He has given us victory over death and shown us His love and mercy through hard times.

Let God fix your dreams. Turn it loose. Let go. He is Our Awesome God. Anything you are not willing to release, He cannot fix because you have not given Him control. Once you put those concerns or worries in His hands, then stand on the Word and watch Him do it. Test, try and prove Him. He is that Word that is alive and real to your heart.

You know how your little ones say, "Mine." You couldn't please the Lord anymore than to say "Mine" about His promises. There's enough to go around for everyone. So encourage yourself and as many others as you can with His Word and your testimony

34

Fight the Good Fight

While we were gone to see family, I received a call on my cell phone from a young man I met at Walmart. He would come through my line every now and then and had quite a struggle there for a while. He had walked close with the Lord and he began to get sick and attack after attack dragged him down.

The caller had been warring for someone he didn't even know. A young woman had been shot with a shotgun and the Lord put such a burden on him that he could not even leave his house until he was released by the Lord. When he called me, I was sitting in the living room of my niece, who was preparing supper for us in Lake Charles, Louisiana. He was so excited. He had been praying for two days and calling in troops to be in corporate agreement with him.

This is a man who had been tossed to and fro by sickness, divorce and had been veritably isolated from people. He could not work because he was attacked by illness when he least expected it. He finally got disability and was able to get his groceries, but to others all this would seem as if he wasn't doing what the Lord wanted and he was being punished. I would compare this to a molding and making, a trying of his faith, if you will. He sounded as if he were going through the Job syndrome.

Now I know people don't always look at things like I do, but there have been times when I have been there and the weight of my situations lay heavily on me, to a disastrous degree of pain. I never lost my smile, because—I know Who my Redeemer is. He has always been in the business of rescuing me, just as he did this young man.

My friend told me he had really needed to go to town, but when he heard about this young mother, in serious condition, with two or three children, God put her on his heart as a prayer warrior. Once he began, he could not stop. When he heard that she was out of danger, the Lord released him from his vigil.

How awesome to have God assign someone to you when you don't even know them. I have even heard of God sending someone to tell a saint the answer to a prayer from a dream in the last year. The woman had been praying for her grandson who was having seizures and she was travailing, weeping intensely to the point of pain in her own body, so severely over the young child. The Lord sent a man in her dreams to tell her that it was the paint glue the child was working with to build his models. With that assurance, she called her son and asked him if her grandson was building models and to ask the doctors to check for allergies to the glue; it was and they were able to bring the seizures under control.

If you have a battle going on in your life, God has the answer. All those years of mom and dad telling you about the Lord and how He used to do things, He still does and He would love to answer your prayers. He loves you as much as He does this man and the woman injured by gunshot. He loves you enough to tell someone somewhere to pray for you. They are merely obeying God. God has His visiting angels all about us of which we are unaware. Remember what you have heard all your life. It is not scriptural, but it is literal: *"God works in mysterious ways."* And, so He does.

This reminds me of a Scripture about Philip. *"And the angel of the Lord spake unto Philip, saying, 'Arise and go toward the south unto the way that goeth down from Jerusalem unto Gaza, which is desert.'"* He went there to meet an Ethiopian eunuch and to lead him to Christ. When the eunuch had been baptized, *"the Spirit of the Lord caught away Philip, that the eunuch saw him no more: and he went on his way rejoicing. But Philip was found at Azotus:"* Acts *8:26 through 38* tell the tale.

Time and space are in the Lord's realm. He is able to do anything to get your needs taken care of. How great is that? I know of people who trust for little things and big things; He answers both.

I know that all things are common to humanity. The things that happened years ago are similar to the things that overtake us now. God healed and delivered back in Bible days.

The late Katherine Kuhlman was a mighty woman of God and she prayed for God to use her mightily and He did. There are people who walk among us who trust God and when He speaks, they have to obey. They have to be responsive to pray or speak words of faith to others. God's love for us is as great as it ever was, if not greater. He is recruiting us for HIS ARMY through rigorous regimentation. He wants us to cover each other with prayer. He wants us to cover each other's back like the Roman soldiers did when they fought. Their armor had no back. Reach out to give encouragement.

Your battle is the Lord's. *If God be for you, who can be against you?* Be a good soldier. Fight that good fight of faith.

35

The Fruit of The Spirit

"But the fruit of the Spirit is love, joy, peace, longsuffering, gentleness [kindness], goodness, faith [faithfulness], meekness, temperance: against such there is no law." - Galatians 5:22-23.

There are nine fruits in this listing, falling from the single, spiritual tree. Jesus said, *"I am the vine, you are my branches."* This fruit is the product of having a real and ongoing relationship with Jesus Christ. A person who comes to Christ and receives His salvation and has a true turn-around experience, a conversion, so to speak, receives the "fruit" of the Spirit. We Christians have been called "fruits" by outsiders. Well, they are absolutely right. We are to be virtuously fruitful!

This **love** is not the kind that is a spontaneous flash in the pan, erotic-type love. It is the love that carries you through the tough times, the roller coaster ride, the highs and lows, the ups and downs of life. Love is what helps a soldier go back for a comrade when they are both in danger and one can't make it by himself. Love is a husband or wife who stands by their mate through thick and thin, through sickness—until death parts them. It is the ingredient that

132

glues two people together into a real, lasting relationship. It is the adhesive that attaches you to Jesus.

His love for you is what nailed Him to the tree, to suffer and die for you. Love is not a fly-by-night emotional high, but has the depth and height and breadth to make it through the terrible times to the terrific times.

<u>Joy</u> is happiness and more. It is a quality of life. As you are stripped of your layers, such as pleasure and contentment and peace of mind, the bottom layer that is unmovable and unshakable is joy. It comes from the soul of the person who has found the *"joy unspeakable and full of glory."* There is nothing plastic or phony or veneered, it is who you are in Christ. Jesus said, *"Be of good cheer [cheerful], I have overcome the world [I am your Overcomer]."*

<u>Peace</u> is the knowing down in your "knower" that God has it all under control. The presence of peace in one's soul helps you to get through a very tumultuous time with the knowledge that whatever happens, the Lord will see you through. Where there is peace, there is no turmoil. A storm could be raging outside your home but the Lord is speaking to your heart and telling you that He is the calm in the midst—you have nothing to fear.

It goes on and on, fruit after fruit. You do get the idea. This fruit is much to be sought after. They are attainable or they would not be mentioned in New Testament Scripture.

When you talk about fruit, something has been planted, right? You hear about the "seed" of the Gospel. *"Faith comes by hearing and hearing by the word of God."* If your heart is fertile ground, the seed takes root and begins to grow until it bears fruit. So, it is a natural 'growing" process in the Lord. As you mature, you naturally become a fruit-bearing plant. *"The fruit falls not far from the tree."* Others pick up the fruit and *"taste and see that it is good."* The seed of the fruit is re-planted and new growth takes place. This is one reason why the Kingdom of God remains until Jesus comes because of the fruitfulness of His saints; fruit begats or bears more fruit.

When the fruit is produced in your spirit by the Holy Spirit, vices are vanquished! There is no longer the anger or hunger for drugs or alcohol or a tendency to be cruel to others, but a tenderness to be like the gentle Savior. It is not trite to say that JESUS IS THE ANSWER. The planting of the seed of the Gospel does produce *love, joy, peace, longsuffering, gentleness, goodness, faith, meekness and temperance.*

Longsuffering means that my mom could suffer long with the things she went through with her family as a young lady and still love them.

She married young to a man that did not love her, then left her when she got pregnant. Her family strongly coerced her to abort the baby. She lived with that regret all her life, but she forgave her family—that's love. Goodness meant she could still be good to them when they were not good to her. She was grateful for all the Lord did for her.

After my dad accepted the Lord, when my brothers were in high school, he became temperate and abstained from drinking. I didn't know the drinking daddy, but my brothers did. They experienced the anger, the hardship and rejection and they loved him anyway; they learned from mama.

The fruit that is produced in the heart of a believer are these and you can tell a believer to be a believer without even asking. The fruit of the Spirit is produced from the residency of Christ in our hearts. People who knew us before, look and say, *"What happened to you? You aren't down at Joe's pool hall anymore. You aren't hanging out at the same old places."* The answer: *"There is no rotten fruit falling from this tree. The old me is dead!"*

36

Happiness in Your New Year

Praise the Lord, we made it this far. We're going through 2017 and have survived. The One Who got us here has another year planned out for us to walk through. As usual, out with the old year and in with the new. Father time, as they say, continues to march on, but it is God Who keeps blessing.

135

Let me announce: this is the year the Lord has made. *I will rejoice and be glad in it.* I will trust in Him "before all else fails." I will praise the Lord.

I can't tell you what the future holds, but I can tell you Who holds the future. He has changed the course of events at His Advent over 2000 years ago. Notice there is "before" the Christ and "after" the Christ on our calendar. He is the pivotal point in human history. He is the changer of individual human lives so as for one to testify, if they have had their conversion, *"This was my life before Christ, now this is my life after Christ. I am a changed person. Nothing is the same since He came into my life."*

He has transformed the ho-hum, hum-drum, unexciting existence of everyday living to: *"He has done so much for me today, what can I do for Him today, tomorrow, the next day and the next?"* And, with Him, there is always tomorrow.

Yes, the Bible says we are not promised tomorrow, but we don't have to live like we have been decreed a death sentence.

One day, we will wake up to a new morning where it is our last tomorrow and it will be "today" forever. It will go on and on and on. It gives us hope for tomorrow and the day after that and the year after that until the tomorrows and the days and the years are gone and it will be an eternity ahead with no worry about the "morrow".

Oh, yes. I got ahead of myself. That previous subject tended to "turn me on." About today, the end of the year, the Holiday Season, the period of time when we all reflect and wish to "resolve" and "absolve" ourselves. This last age is getting older. Let me explain. According to theologians, this is the "church" age, the last period before the return of our Lord. I am not saying that this is or isn't the end of time; but as you read your Bible and the newspaper, all indications are that we are nearing the END. The signs are becoming more and more apparent. Don't get overly alarmed.

The averages have it that we will reach 2012. But, we do need to face a reality that things are wrapping up and winding down. I am saying that in this "end time," we must *look to the hills [highest places] from whence cometh my (our) help my (our) help cometh from the Lord."* There I go with the calm of *Psalms121*; as a matter of fact.

Another comforting Psalm is *Psalms 91:1-2, 11-12.* "He *that dwelleth in the secret place of the Most High shall abide under the shadow of the Almighty. I will say of the Lord, He is my refuge and my fortress: my God; in Him will I trust . . . For He shall give His angels charge over thee, to keep thee in all thy ways. They shall bear thee up in their hands, lest thou dash thy foot against a stone."*

I want you to be hopeful; in other words, full-of-hope for the New Year. God has given us the hope that is in His Son, Jesus Christ, Whom He sent to deliver us out of the hands of death, Hell and the grave. Yes, we may lay in a grave for a time, but the grave can't hold us if we know Christ!

We need to get ready for an awesome adventure. This kind of attitude gives us more altitude. We need to plant these seeds of positive faith as we go into time of newness.

God is on our side. It is a New Year and a new leaf to be turned over. What is in the past, we should leave behind us. In our house growing up, we all turned over a new leaf in every sense of the word and started over every year. We forgave each other and planned to make a new start for the next year and quit the old things that were not suitable or acceptable in our lives.

God's pledge is true and He is coming again. No man knows the day nor the hour, but everyone has a sense of some great event coming.

If you talk to a tribe in the bush of South America, Africa, Australia or the farthest islands in the Seven Seas, they know something is going to happen. Jesus said He would return and I believe.

Even after referencing the world's current events, Jesus remains the Advocate. He has watched, saved, healed, and delivered souls from drugs, alcohol and varied other self-destructive habits, giving many a new chance. He is still keeping His promise that if you will accept Him, the old person will pass away, this is not dying physically, but your spirit becomes new. He holds us near and dear to His heart; He has a place prepared for us.

Here is the slogan for the New Year: *"We will higher delve in the year Twenty-twelve"* or whatever year you read this. Have a happy one. Be safe and secure in Him. May all your blessings abound in the upcoming. Be it known I have been blessed to be of service to you. God bless you, one and all. I love you all, with the love of Jesus Christ.

37

How Did It Feel?

We all talk about feelings. We've all got some. How about the song many of us older folks remember, *"feelings, whoa . . . oh . . . o-o-o . . . feel - - - ings!"* I'll bet you can almost hear me singing it now. How about the question we ask each other casually, continuously, *"How are you feeling today?"* My Dad would say he was feeling with his fingers. That's a haha.

There is a question I would like to ask you right now in which I really want you to search your soul for the answer. How did it feel when you first found Jesus? Did your heart feel clean and pure? Did you feel as if your heart was soaring into the heights of Heaven and it wasn't your time to go yet? Did you have the feeling of exquisite peace? Was it a feeling that was nearly indescribable? You just had a feeling that you had never felt before?

When I was a child of eight years old, I accepted Christ. I didn't feel anything except the drawing of the Holy Spirit when I knew I needed to go to the front of the church. It was as if an invisible hand was pulling at my heartstrings to lead me forward. I felt the Holy Spirit saying to my heart, *"Come."* Another way to describe it is if someone grabs your shirt and pulls at you, only—the pull was inside. I followed His leading and asked Jesus Christ into my heart. I remember telling the pastor that I felt like I needed Jesus.

I remember learning *John 3:16* before the age of eight. Even someone that never darkens the doors of a church can almost literally quote this verse. You'll see someone holding high a sign referencing that verse in every professional football game. The reason for the recognition of that verse is that it is the Gospel in a nutshell. Why, in a sense, if you get it, you get it all. *"For God loved the [whole-wide] world that He gave . . . [a GIFT] . . . . ., His Only begotten Son, who gave us eternal life When we leave this life, this isn't all there is.*

It should not be overlooked that even at my early age of eight, I had my doubters. My mother made sure that I knew what I was doing and the minister counselled me several times before I was baptized. My pastor's name was

Brother Erwin and he made sure I knew what I was doing.

Let's talk some more about that experience. Maybe, when you were in your first day of that exciting moment with Almighty God, you felt like you was seeing the world in a new light, like the heavens opened up to you. Nothing was the same anymore, especially in your heart. Maybe, it's like feeling alive for the first time. It is true that when the "spirit person" is turned on, you are feeling a side of yourself that has been dormant for many, many years. You had felt the body and mind and emotion of yourself, but never the soul and spirit of yourself. This sensation is something you are unaccustomed to.

In *John 1:6* implies that Jesus is the light of the world, the light that lights all men and the darkness cannot seize it. There are a lot of dark places in this world presently. Without Christ it would be even darker.

Saul witnessed the light of Christ as a blinding presence on the road to Damascus *(Acts 9:4-6)*. Jesus gave Peter peace while raging waves rocked the boat when he stepped out onto the water in faith to come to Him. When the earth was darkened and quaked at the death of Christ on the cross on Calvary's hilltop, the Roman soldier shouted out, *"Truly, this is the Son of God!"* Sometimes, it takes "seeing the light."

It is not enough to just waddle through this life with no

direction and no drive. Christ gives purpose and strength He gives you the ability to overcome and make something special of yourself.

It takes some feeling to get into the game, but it is faith that is the game changer, not feeling. If we acted solely on the way we feel, we would only get things half-done. When we walk by faith, things are fully finished. Paul the Apostle stated, *"I have fought a good fight; I have finished the course."* There is the "feeling factor" that will shine through after accepting Christ.

The young girl who professed Jesus Christ in front of the young assailants at Columbine did not go on feelings alone on that fateful day. She knew that her expression of faith might cause her death. And, so it did. They made an example of her by killing her. But her testimony still stands.

In this world of ours, every child seems to have to grow up faster. Growth in the Lord gives one immeasurable maturity. When I found Him at eight, I grew up always wanting more of the Lord.

Well, I have been here, there and everywhere. I have probably been around the world once or twice with this article. I'm not sure why you keep reading my words. You indicate at my place of employment that you read them consistently. It may be that you feel what I feel. I know that I feel for others. You sure can't take the feelings out of living. Beyond that, when you fortify your feelings with faith, you become a "powerhouse."

Do you have the same feelings for the Lord that you had in the very beginning?

From the child of eight years old to the woman of seventy-two, I want to grow more in Him daily—and I do. I have a heart for the Lord, the heart of a child, and for those who want to know more about Him. He is as concerned about the child in the womb as He is an old woman like me.

How did it feel for me? Peace. He gave me peace to face loss of parents, divorce, loss of friends, many trials as an adult and brought me this far to walk in the love of Jesus Christ.

If you've never experienced that, you still have time. As long as there is breath in your body, there is hope. There is no other feeling like it. It's like being high on hope! Find it, feel it, live it. It is exhilarating. Come on, try it. You'll like it.

Step in, the water's fine.

38

How Many Times Will God Bless Us?

If you will remember in another article, I mentioned that I am here after three generations of my people moving to Texas. I didn't know a whole lot about us, but my mom's step dad would always talk to her about those Tennessee Walking Horses. He talked about those horses, the Tennessee moon and the Tennessee Waltz.

Since I moved here from Texas to Tennessee, I have experienced blessing after blessing. Several years ago, now, a blessing came through a couple, who have known Kent through his shop and me through Walmart. They read the article about Tennessee Walking Horses, and blessed us with tickets to the Show in Shelbyville. Have you ever seen a Racking horse that can walk and never break into a gallop at thirty-five miles per hour? Did you know the walking horses learn to walk in that high stepping manner by wearing an ankle bracelet and pads on their feet? The whole spectacle was spectacularly good!

We greatly appreciated that experience and the introduction to the Tennessee Walking Horses. My Momma would have loved seeing that and I texted all our kids to show them what we were seeing. It was some show and what a blessing. We want to extend our heartfelt thanks to the couple who gave us those tickets and for the opportunity to experience the Horses and learn more about a wonderful Tennessee pastime and heritage.

It was pretty warm, scorching, there in Shelbyville. No breeze. Everyone had something to fan with, but it wasn't as bad as Texas.

It appeared as if Tropical Storm Lee would bring relief to Texas, but it didn't. If anything, it brought more misery. Lee created winds that moved the fires back and forth between communities near my two daughters' homes.

I talked to my younger daughter and the fire that had destroyed 8,000 acres was 12 miles from their town. My older daughter told me that her husband was having to work late and you could smell the fires all around. There were fires not too far to the east and then to the west. My son said that a day or two before there was a fire some three miles or more from their house. The fire department stopped that one right across the street from an apartment complex and a subdivision in San Antonio. The girls live near Houston.

My younger daughter was headed home from work on a Wednesday as we made our way to church. She was driving right by a great roaring fire to get home. I told her we were going to put her on the prayer list and she said, *"Thanks, mom."* In the course of conversation, she said she didn't want to give up everything she had worked for and I told her that the same God Who had spared her from having to go canoeing down the Guadalupe under duress would take care of her and her family in this situation. I told her, *"When it gets too heavy, hand it to the Lord. He will carry it for you and He will help you through it."* She responded with *"Okay, mom."*

This is the same young woman who had a tree by her house during Hurricane Rita and she just knew it would fall on her house and I told her that I would ask God to put a great big angel there to guard the house. If the tree fell, it would fall the other way, and it did.

Blessings come in all shapes and sizes, from tickets to a Horse Show to God protecting your children and a tree falling away from their house. They come in the form of getting you through the day at a job that is almost intolerable, to a sickness that is working on getting you down.

My response to those situations is to strike back with praise to the Lord and He will inhabit the area around you. He may bring you tickets from out of the blue because someone found out that you had a childhood dream or He may guard your family through tough times.

I was praying that Tropical Storm Lee would give the kids some relief in Texas and definitely wreaked havoc in the north with flood waters destroying homes and lives. Now we've had Harvey hit in 2017 and Irma doesn't know where she is going. Signs of the times are all around us. It may not be hours and it may not be days, but the return of Christ is nearer than before and you can see the prophecies in the Word coming to pass with *wars and rumors of wars*. God is not too busy to bless His children in the midst of such events.

In *Deuteronomy 28:2*, it says, *"And all these blessings shall come on thee, and overtake thee, if thou shalt hearken unto the voice of the Lord thy God."* Just like that beautiful Racking horse at the Show. That horse breezed around that track. Your blessings, if you are obedient to the Lord as stipulated in *verse 2*, are coming up on you and overtaking you. You can't outrun your blessings and they propel you to the finish line.

I would say there are plenty more blessings before us. As long as there is life, God is in the blessing business. He loved us from the first breath He put it in Adam and will bless us until the last breath man and woman take.

39

How Stubborn Am I

Sometimes you have things happen in your life that raise questions and you have a head scratching experience? Well, I had that a while back.

We had a wonderful brother in the Lord pass away due to Cancer and his wife had to give away their dog. She was going to have to move into an apartment and downsize and she couldn't take a hyper 2 year old border collie with her.

Border Collies are trained to herd and be outside and we built her a pen. Well we picked her up and brought her to Crossville. She wrestled a little because she wanted to sit in the front seat or on my husband's shoulder.

She didn't like a leash or a harness or a tether, but we didn't want to sacrifice her to the many who had been run over on the road. We had a pen built for her before she got here. She had a shed on one end and we put her food by the gate.

Well, we left the harness on her and she would wrestle when we put the leash on, but treats were soon introduced to the relationship.

I walked her a few times and Kent walked her more than I. We got a tether and she enjoyed sitting out in the sun, but when leash time came, she did every move in the book to get free.

I hit the ground four different times in four weeks. The first time she got out of her harness somehow and I was trying to help Kent keep her still to get the leash on her and sat down abruptly when I didn't want to. She nipped at his hands and we got the leash back on. A couple of days later, she tripped me and I fell to my knees. That didn't happen for another 5 days or so and I landed on the ground face first yelling at Kent to get her. I had her by one finger holding the harness and I didn't know how long that would last. Then the following Saturday, she and I had a tussle and my glasses went one way and I landed on top of her because of her dodging the leash again. She tripped me, I went down on top of her and that catastrophe was a blessing because she had pulled loose from the leash. I walked her and applied my, supposed to be, training techniques and walked about ten feet and hooked her back up to the tether and went in the house.

Kent said we would go walking later and I said I would go with him. We walked over our 2.3 acre yard.

Well, Sunday morning came and we were looking forward to getting out there to feed her and my husband made the discovery. Everything had just gotten more complicated. We were ready for church and she had gotten loose. She climbed that four foot sturdy fence and was out. We had people waiting to go with us to church and here we were chasing her and she had chewed the harness halfway in two.

I ran and got treats and she responded. She acted as though she was going to do a run by and take a finger or two and would dodge me when I would try to grab her, but finally she got the treat and I got her. She actually walked back to the pen and I got her leash chained to the gate.

Well, knowing that the harness was halfway in two, we had to leave anyway and had done all we knew to do. She met us happily when we got home from church, but we didn't see her again until Monday morning laying in our back yard, dead. Sad story and I really miss her but I watched what was going on between us. The only thing we could figure out was that she has herding cows in her blood and she went to the pasture behind us and one of the cows kicked her and she brought herself back to our home and died. She must have felt we were home for her. It wasn't a very happy event, but what time we had her, chasing her or not we loved her dearly.

I correlated that to our stubbornness with God. I wonder if He gets as frustrated with us as I did with this beautiful animal that was our rough little friend for a while.

I'm reminded of a Scripture that tells us this, *"My son, despise not the chastening of the Lord; neither be weary of his correction: For whom the Lord loveth he corrupteth; even as a father the son is when he delighteth." - Proverbs 3:11-12.*

Let us not be stubborn towards our heavenly Father when He is trying do something to help us through our lives. Being stubborn makes it harder for us to see what the Lord has done and is doing for us. We are a lot like 'Pretty Girl' in that we don't want to be corrected or tied down.

We must sit at the feet of Jesus and listen to that still small Voice. He will teach us, if we let Him and He will give us what we need. I have been stubborn and it is not fun. *"He will supply all our needs according to His riches in Glory through Christ Jesus."*

150

I pray I am not so stubborn that He has to chase me down, tackle me and make me mind. Of course, God is a gentleman and gives us a choice of whether or not to serve Him. I choose to serve the Lord.

40

It's Seasonal

"To every thing there is a season, and a time to every purpose under the heaven; A time to be born, and a time to die; a time to plant, and a time to pluck up that which is planted; A time to kill, and a time to heal; . . . A time to weep, and a time to laugh; a time to mourn, and a time to dance; . . . A time to get, and a time to lose; a time to keep, and a time to cast away; a time to keep silence, and a time to speak; A time to love, and a time to hate; a time of war, and a time of peace." - Ecclesiastes 3:1-8

All this sounds deeply profound, but it all still holds true that there is a time and season for everything. Fall fell abruptly this last weekend and told us in its own unspoken language that one shouldn't get too comfortable in this in-between stage. It has some things to show you. With thirty to forty degrees at night and fifty to sixty during the day, we got the message. Winter will be here soon.

I have a praise in that I won't be having to drive up and down the Plateau in bad weather this winter. I have retired and am learning a new schedule wrapped up in my husband, home, church and family; I'm doing some quilting, and a new great grandchild will be here in November.

We had to get the Michigan trip done before it got too cold and the roads got too bad for Kent's eighty-five year old mom to travel. It got in the thirties at night there and we began feeling it. Mom had to go see her seventy-nine year old sister. It was fun and they started talking as soon as we got there and didn't stop 'til we left. It was a time of refreshing and catching up on things. The "Remember When's" were hashed and rehashed. So, we made the trip before things would change dramatically—the one constant is change.

Change is coming on a large scale with this campaign season that will last more than a year. If it's not one thing, it is another to try our very souls. What we are looking for is character in candidates. But, individuals seem to change more than the seasons. I don't like politics and don't enjoy the rhetoric of the stump. I do see the promises of change that are floating around the airwaves into our hearts and minds. Our futures are at stake. I've heard it for decades. It is a truism. *"I don't know my future but I know who holds my future because He holds my future and holds my hand!"*

With God's help, the changes that come will be for our good and not our bad, just as with His help, we will handle this winter well with the ice and the snow that will come, a near certainty. But we can be assured that *Romans 8: 28* will kick into affect. It tells us *"all things work together for our good, whether we see it or we don't"*.

In an even larger scale, the 32 year old minister named Youcef, who stands in peril in Iran needs our prayers. Many of us say, *"How can that affect us?"* and we don't see that this is something that we may very well face in our own time. Our faith will be tested if Jesus tarries. For many, it already has. Don't overlook that change is in the air. This international climate indicates to me that *"perilous times"* are pending. Our hearts will be tried and only time will tell whether our faith or the lack thereof will be exposed.

Our faith in God will get us through this season on every level from our personal family to the global family that affect us near and dear to our hearts. What the Iranian Christian is facing may some day be our lot. What does our heart say? Who do we believe? As for me and my house, we believe and serve the living God. Jesus saved my soul many years ago. That seed was planted and took root at the age of 8. Jesus carried me through valleys and onto mountaintops that make me who I am. I still grow daily at 66 years of age. My character and how I live as *"unto the Lord"* has a spiritual effect on my children and grandchildren. I can affect change to a positive degree within my sphere. I know that my prayers uplift others and I see them answered, not because of who I am, but because of Who Christ is in me. I have made a personal pledge to never change!

The change is seasonal, my friends. The winds of change are swirling around us and we need to be ready for whatever comes. Hold on tight to Jesus and hear Him calling you to stay close to Him. He will keep you wrapped in His arms through tears and laughter, the wind and the cold, the sunshine and the rain. Listen for that *"still small voice"* that whispers PEACE to the core of your being in the midst of stormy changes.

"Be still and peaceful."

41

My Walmart Chapter Has Closed

With a fond farewell, I said goodbye to 11 years, 1 month and 24 days of working at Walmart. June 27th, 2010 closed one chapter and opened another. I had just turned 66 years of age.

This was hard because of my intense emotional involvement in this arena of public life. When I moved to Crossville two plus years ago, I could have transferred to the Crossville Walmart, but I was ready for retirement. I have told everybody in Crossville that my friends are at the

Cookeville store. My friends were a constant encouragement to me every day on the job. My other friends were the customers, some of who came through my line consistently. My second language is Spanish which draws the Hispanic crowd to my counter. So, I have friends everywhere. Some made my day when they told me about their enjoyment of the articles I had in the local paper. Get this: even those who didn't agree with me were kind enough to express their views.

I will continue writing, but that may not be as often. I wake up some mornings with an idea that won't turn me loose. I get to the computer and it is right for the hour. I found out with its publication that it hit someone at their point of great need.

Everybody knows I am a highly emotional writer anyway. It was with great and grievous emotion that I said goodbye to all the customers and coworkers. It was fun. How many people can say that? There'd been times that some of my friends at Walmart stood with me, such as when my husband was sick, when I had surgery, when my son had Cancer, praying with me for all my needs to be taken care of by the Lord Who is our only real strength in daily living.

People had come through my line day in and day out for 6 or 7 years and before that for some four years or so as a greeter, expecting a smile or expecting a *"How do you do?"* They were not disappointed for the most part. I have learned from the customers with all manner of actions and reactions, more positive than not.

I found many friends throughout those years and am grateful for the opportunities of making friends and acquaintances. I watched kids grow up and have kissed many a baby's little head and little toes. Maybe, I could have run for office and didn't know it.

I came away with a plethera of memories. Often, I was used as an interpreter for the Spanish only speaking folks. I gained as many Spanish friends as Anglo. My abilities to speak differently ranged from English to Spanish to German, learned in school back in Texas in the 60's. I was always trying to learn more. I learned a few words in Mandarin Chinese, Japanese, Hebrew, Arabic, Bosnian, Malayalam (an Indian language as in India) to greetings in Lakota and Apache . . . all of this from the door as a greeter. Just a word of greeting was all it took sometimes to gain a smile.

I love people and I love building bridges to reach their hearts. Many responded positively when I could speak merely a word of their native tongue. I have always felt that if I went to another country I would hope I would find someone who spoke my language and I would be comforted in my visit to a foreign land.

I have a story about the Malayalam language, a dialect of an Indian language which I hope I spelled correctly. I learned how to say *"God bless you"* in that language some 16 or so years ago, working in Houston. One day I asked a young Indian woman if she could understand what I was saying and said the phrase exactly. She almost welled up in tears and said, *"Yes, that is my language. How do you know this?"* I explained how and her appreciation was unmeasured. It brightened my day to brighten hers. She said she had needed that blessing at the time and was so grateful for the experience.

Here's another story about a man from Arabia who taught me how to greet in his language. An older man had come to visit his son who attended Tennessee Tech and he had a problem with his heart. He came in one day and there was not a motorized cart. He was with his grandson and took off without waiting for a cart and one came in right after he walked away. He was too far away to get his attention so I got someone to take my place at the door took off on the motorized cart and caught up with him. He bowed and put his hand on his heart in thanks. I later asked his son how to greet his father and learned a blessing for the older man when he would come to visit. He had the biggest grin when he would come in, building another bridge.

There are countless stories in the wild world of Walmart, but every day was an experience with some outstanding person or character. There have been more people than characters in my little corner of the world and I have really enjoyed all of you who made my day with your contact and conversation.

My Spanish friends who would first hear me speak in their native tongue were usually very surprised that I could communicate. They were always a joy to serve, as well.

Then there is my German experience. An older man who had a restaurant and I would always speak a little German. Several would come through and I would practice what I had learned in high school. Then there is the couple who come from Germany twice a year to visit their daughter (Brother Bobby Davis' wife), and would always come in the store to speak to me from halfway around the world. They would bring their grandson and he was amazed that I could speak his language.

Romans 8:28 says: *"For we know that all things work together for the good of them that love the Lord which are called according to His purpose."* The Lord did me good at Walmart. I leave with many work friends and many counter friends. What can I say? It has been a pleasure. You will never be forgotten. You are in my daily prayer. I know . . . I was slurpy and sniffly and syrupy and sloppy. You only say goodbye once. I wanted to go out with a "hoot and a holler." I sure got a lot of bang with my buck at Walmart! Maybe, this will go national. How many people have said goodbye glowingly to the biggest department store chain in the world.

I was truly grateful for the opportunity and still am after 7 years of retirement. Thank you, Lord, and bless them all. I will continue to write. You will still hear from me occasionally. There are baby quilts to make, newsletters to write, paintings to be painted.

"Muchado" (much to do) for something. God bless you, one and all.

42

Nehemiah Builds the Wall

I recently heard that a tunnel was completed through the Alps in Switzerland, 51 miles long completely through the Alps. It was opened with a full demonic ceremony dedicating it to Satan. Along with this there is a huge machine that one of the very scientists who invented it said we've done something we shouldn't. I know it's not in our part of the world, but all these things affect us.

If a tunnel can be built in honor of Satan, why can't he tear down our churches?

God's been dealing with me about walls. Not tunnels so much [even though illegal aliens tunnel through our borders], but the walls are in our church and must come down so that the walls of our church building in Baxter can be completed.

We are doing battle, brothers and sister, we are doing battle within the Church. The enemy doesn't want God's Word to be spread throughout the world.

Nehemiah 1:4 says, "And it came to pass, when I heard these words, that I sat down and wept, and mourned certain days, and fasted, and prayed before the God of heaven, What words were these?, the wall of Jerusalem also is broken and the gates thereof are burned with fire."

It is just as if we were in that shape within our individual churches. The remnant that are left of the captivity there in the province are in great affliction and reproach:

Nehemiah was more upset about the wall because he knew how vulnerable they were. The people out there are vulnerable, they don't have Jesus Christ, *Yeshua Hamashia*. Many know they need something, but they don't really know what it is that they need to fill the void in their souls.

King Ataxerxes saw that Nehemiah was troubled and asked Nehemiah, his cupbearer, what was wrong and Nehemiah told him. The king gave him the time off he needed to travel to Jerusalem and see to the task. He gave him letters to the governors beyond the river. Nehemiah was a favored man of God.

At the same time there were two men who were highly upset that Nehemiah was planning to work on the walls, Sanballat the Horonite and Tobiah the servant, the Ammonite and they were grieved that Nehemiah was planning to work on the wall.

There were nine gates, <u>1st the sheep gate</u>—representing God's people;

<u>2nd there was the fish gate</u>—representing souls; <u>3rd and old gate</u>—representing the foundation; <u>4th the valley gate</u>—representing the people wounded, broken and backslidden; <u>5th the dung gate</u>—representing the garbage out of the body after going through the valley; <u>6th the gate of the fountain</u>—pure water flowing after cleansing; <u>7th the Water gate</u>—flow trickling as a stream of, the river; <u>8th the Horse gate</u>—flow from the touch of the Lord's power; and <u>9th the East gate</u> —The second coming.

Different families were assigned the different gates and families were assigned sections in between the gates.. It started off with Eliashib the high priest who rose up with his brethren the priests and they built the sheep gate; they sanctified it and set up the doors of it; even unto the tower of Meah they sanctified it, unto the tower of Hananeel.

And next unto him, the men of Jericho. Family or towns or groups of men stood and worked side by side.

I watch the Mennonites and what I have heard of the Amish, in a day like today, they still raise barns, they work together after all these generations, they still know how to work together to build what they have in their hearts to do for a neighbor and we are looking at the house of God in Baxter.

I may be 72, but I am merely a child. I am taking my harp off the Cedar. I have to be obedient to the Lord. I've preached in jails with Carol's sister and in black churches and shared in Spanish churches and sung. I stand here today *with God's Word shut up in my bones like fire.*

In *Nehemiah 4*, Sanballat and Tobiah, mocked the Jews and said what these feeble Jews think they can do? They won't be able to build a strong wall, even the foxes will be able to break down their stone wall.

Nehemiah answers by prayers in *Nehemiah 4:4—5 and in verse 6, So built we the wall.*

They took turns working side by side and guarding each other as they sought to please the Lord in rebuilding the wall of Jerusalem.

Okay, maybe we don't do it that way anymore, but we do have to guard each other, We need to guard each others backs as though we were in war like the Romans, they stood back to back because they had no armor. We need to pray for each other and lift each other up and Praise God for bringing in the lost sheep. We need to go after the ninety and nine.

There've been more than one who have seen visions of the people who will throng to the Church in this great revival. There is to be A GREAT REVIVAL that is to come before Christ returns. I don't want blood on my hands, by being slack in what we need to do to bring in those who have been spurned by the Church and brokenhearted. There are lost people out there who are counting on God's people. Even those who have laughed and mocked us (like the Jews were) need to see God's people rise up in His strength and power to touch hearts and lives.

Now let's deal with the walls in our congregations, in our churches. We know they are there, but we don't address them.

I was told once, some thirty-five years or more, that I was like Rachel weeping for her children. Sometimes that's you, your heart, your health, and your needs. We have a little lady who is praying for her family and she refuses to give up and I stand in agreement with her for their souls.

Let's address these walls, the boo-boos or hurts I see. Remember when your babies would come say, *"Mommy, I have a boo-boo, I hurt? I fell down."* Many of our walls may come from childhood on up, but we need to deal with them today so we can move on from here.

I see sensitiveness, confusion, doubt, indecision, pride, competition, bitterness, rebellion, strife, control, accusation, rejection, insecurity, jealousy, escape or indifference, passivity (or passive), depression, gloom, heaviness, generational curses of Daddy didn't do it that way, unforgiveness. If we don't forgive one another, God will not forgive us. (I want His forgiveness and if I have offended any one of you forgive me) He says this in *1 John*.

Python is a spirit that wraps around the members of the Church and whispers in their ears. This vile spirit from the pits of Hell says you can't do this, you know you aren't good enough, you can't give that money or you won't have enough money to make your bills. You can't teach or you can't please God, look what you did last week.

That's all a mouthful, but it is here and,

"By the blood of Jesus Christ I say to these strong men that hold our churches captive (spiritual strong men), I curse you to the root and cast you to the bottom of the sea. Father I ask You to replace these evil hindering spirits with a double portion of Your Holy Spirit that by the stripes of Jesus Christ, Son of the Most High God in Jesus' Name our churches be healed!

"I ask that You replace these with forgiveness, peace, joy, faith security in You and Love for our brothers and our sisters. Father, help us pull together and build our churches and build the Body. Open our ears to You and help us to be a blessing to one another and Your humble servants. We love You Lord and praise You for victory in this very hour, and that we build the Church for Your glory Honor and praise in Jesus' Name.

And Lord, let us be as Nehemiah about our churches and our country. I ask this in the Name of Jesus Christ."

43

Playing Life as a Game

How many times have people walked up and said, *"How's the world treating you?"* Each time, my response is, *"Not worth a flip, but the Lord just keeps me with blessing after blessing."* It is true, the Creative God of all—is AWE-SOME, but *the god of this world* is the one who *"comes to steal, kill and destroy." (John 10:10)* That Hell-bound god, the enemy to our very souls, wants to rattle our cages and shake us to pieces. It is his goal to make it difficult to be useful to ourselves or anyone else in this world. We war within ourselves as to what is right and wrong.

The only Overseer of the universe watches over us when we wake or sleep (*". . . Now I lay me down to sleep. I pray the Lord my soul to keep . . ."*) and He's the One Who we try to avoid or show blissful ignorance of on many occasions. We try His patience just as our children try to see what they can get by with. Then when we start reaping the rewards of our misdeeds, the realization sets in that we have been caught!

In *Romans 7:15*, Paul wrote of his predicament. *"For that which I do I allow not: for what I would, that do I not; but what I hate, that do I."*

Then, in the same chapter in *Romans, verses 24 through*

165

25, "O wretched man that I am! Who shall deliver me from the body of this death? I thank God through Jesus Christ, our Lord. So then with the mind I myself serve the law of God; but with the flesh the law of sin." That saved, saintly Apostle Paul faced the same dilemma we do today. In my feeble way of thinking, Paul was saying, *"What I want to do that I know is right is intensely overcome by the flesh. That makes me hate myself, but I do it anyway. By pressing myself perpetually to do what is right in the sight of God, righteousness wins out in the end. Thank God."*

Paul was a godly man, but even he was playing the game of life early on. While still Saul, he was doing it his way by persecuting Christians. It was a struggle for him to do what he knew was right and draw away from the earthly folly that tormented him, as well as the rest of us. He was tried by the enemy who would have loved to destroy Paul, but that opposing force could never outdo the truth of God that will ultimately and triumphantly set you free!

Each of us struggles with something at all times. It is a fact of life, if you are not struggling you are not living. We do not always live in a friendly world and often not a fair one either. We make wrong decisions and suffer for them. This is our own self-inflicted punishment. The beauty is we don't have to be repeat offenders. Thank God we generally live another day to brush ourselves off and get back up and begin to make better decisions. That is the graciousness of God towards all of us. *"Okay, son or daughter, stand up, straighten up and start over."* I hear the preacher say all the time, *"He is the God of fresh starts and new beginnings".* Paul was shaky at first; however, what a strong finish.

Life isn't a game, but God gives us a "sporting," spiritual chance to be successful. For example, there is a second-hand thrift store in our mall in Crossville, called Second Chance. It reminds me that many opportunities are given to the unfortunate around us. My husband and I go there fairly often. It begs me to ask the question, *"How many accept a hand, hang on and help themselves?"* If there is failure, where did it go wrong? It is God's desire *that none should perish,* but all should be found and unbound .

There are lots of people in need, but not all are responsive and they like trying to get around the system. To some it is just a game. Their goal is to see how many cookies they can get out of the cookie jar before they get caught. When they are caught, they are not sad they did it, but regret they were caught. They think they are smart enough to outsmart those who have been trained to deal with the discrepancies. Definitely, they can't outsmart or outthink God Almighty. Be aware, every cookie you acquire underhandedly will crumble in your hands.

Life was even compared to a race in *Hebrews 12:1-2b.* *"Wherefore seeing we also are compassed about with so great a cloud of witnesses, let us lay aside every weight, and the sin which doth so easily beset us, and let us run with patience the race that is set before us. Looking unto Jesus the author and finisher of our faith."*

What do we do about the game players? One day the games will be over and those playing life's games will lose. We need to consider ourselves projects not yet finished. Don't play your way through life—do what is right. Life can be full of fun, but it is no game. Don't play games, instead gain through Christ. *The wages of sin is death* and destruction. *The gift of God is life* through Christ. Paul himself spoke it best: *"I HAVE fought a good fight, I HAVE finished the course, I HAVE kept the faith".*

We must trust God for ourselves and walk with a prayer on our lips for others playing games and trying to sneak under the wire. Pray for those involved with drugs or those drinking to excess. Pray for your children and grandchildren. Don't play games, but trust and obey our Lord and Savior. Hold fast to His Word and stand in for those who just don't get it.

44

Something We All Need to Know

One thing we already know is that the Word tells us in Hebrews, *"For the word of God is quick, and powerful, and sharper than any two-edged sword, piercing even to the di-*

viding asunder of soul and spirit,..." Then in *Isaiah 55:11,* it says, *"So shall my word be that goeth forth out of my mouthy: it shall not return unto me void, but it shall accomplish that which I please, and it shall prosper in the thing whereto I sent it."*

Now many of us have learned over the years to pray Scripture and we see results. When I first came here, I learned about a Scripture that would stop bleeding. A friend of mine, Sybil Stuart, had told me about an incident where a dear friend of hers was bleeding through their gums and there was no stopping the flow of blood and she just knew that he would surely die and she found out about this Scripture. The Scripture is *Ezekiel 16:6. "And when I passed by thee, and saw thee polluted in thine own blood, I said unto thee when thou was in thy blood, Live; yea, I said unto thee when thou was in thy blood, Live."* The profuse bleeding stopped. The man died, but not of the intense blood loss. The doctors couldn't understand it. God's Word did what it was sent to do.

Okay, several months ago, the husband of one of our members had a problem with his stomach and he was bleeding a tremendous amount of blood. He had a lesion which had a vessel that was leaking blood in His stomach. They don't know what causes those lesions, it is a medical mystery. They could not stop the bleeding. He had two surgeries within a few days. Pastor asked the woman, do you trust me? She said sure I do. He quoted the Scripture in *Ezekiel 16:6* and the blood ceased to flow. After all was said and done, all the blood was replaced in his body and then some.

Well, then this past Sunday morning, I found out that one of my sisters in the Lord had a complication from surgery she had gone back to the doctor for her check up and they found that she had internal bleeding and had lost at least two or more pints of blood and reminded her about that Scripture. She looked at me with a twinkle in her eye and said she knew. She said that when she thought her granddaughter was bleeding from a four-wheeler accident, she had used it then and it wasn't her granddaughter, it was her.

The report on sister Betty was that she was going to have surgery and she wouldn't be able to do anything for at least six months. She had surgery and went back in two weeks and they said she wouldn't be able to do anything for three months. Well, needless to say, she has trusted the Lord for all that she has been through and He has shown up.

Isn't God amazing? He has given us His Word to heal us.

Oh and Vicky, the keyboard player, has her husband home, fat and I don't think he is sassy. I think he is sure glad to be home with his wife and better. This is living proof that God's Word is powerful. When there is a need—His Word is the key to what is needed.

There's a line in a song that I used to sing, *"The Promise."* *He holds the key to what you need, death and Hell He will defeat. There's a promise coming down your dusty road."*

Who do you depend on? God is the most reliable friend and He loves so much. We are the sheep of His pasture if we have accepted Him. If we haven't, He waits with out-stretched arms and the same love He had for us when He hung on that cross to forgive us of all our sins. He has the same love for us when they beat Him unmercifully to bear the stripes on His back to heal us.

When you are reading the pages of that Bible, you are reading Jesus. Time has not changed Jesus. *He is the same yesterday, today and forever.* His love is the same as it was when He climbed Calvary's hill.

There is power in the Word of God. It is yours to speak when a loved one is hurting. It is yours to comfort you when times are hard. *Ezekiel 16:6* in these unrelated events is something we all need to know.

I know that many of us feel we must try any and all other things and then finally trust God's Word; but if we trust His Word first, we find we suffer far less through this life.

171

45

The Church is a Saving Place

The primary purpose of the Church is to be the going place for folks to grow spiritually. But, also, it must reach outside its walls to grow inside. Bluntly speaking, the drawing card should be the reservoir of love and mercy within. So, why are the number of active participants dwindling? The Bible emphasizes in: *Isaiah 35:4, "Your God will save you"; Luke 7:50,"Thy faith hath saved you"; John 12:47, "For I came not to judge the world, but to save the world."; 1 Timothy 1:15, "This is a faithful saying, and worthy of all acceptation, that Christ Jesus came into the world to save sinners".*

The sinners need saving. Where are they? Out there. Jesus instructed His disciples to *"GO and teach all nations, baptizing them in the Name of the Father, and of the Son, and of the Holy Ghost: teaching them to observe all things whatsoever I have commanded you: and lo, I am with you alway, even unto the end of the world. Amen." - Matthew 28:19-20*

Once they come into the fold, we need to HOLD them. I mean, put your arms around them! In *Jeremiah 23:1*, the shepherds of the flock were warned not to scatter the sheep. They are to gather, not scatter. This law of the Old Testament holds true for the New Testament Church, as well.

Love, love, love people into the Kingdom. *"People are hurting and they need our healing help."* Our job as Christians is to care for them.

Isaiah 35:3 says, *"Strengthen ye the weak hands, and confirm the feeble knees. Say to them that are of a fearful heart, Be strong, fear not: behold, your God will come with vengeance, even God with a recompence; he will come and save you."*

We are all flesh. Sometimes, the way we are treated, even at church, tends to raw the flesh. In that tender state, the body tends to avoid the Church and the church "goers" to lessen the pain. We have taken a "hit" and we don't want to be hit again. The thought needs to be presented that the CHURCH is a walk-in clinic and that soul will receive immediate attention—whatever the condition.

The Holy Spirit is our teacher in the absence of Jesus Christ Who is sitting at the right hand of the Father. I'm asking a serious question.

What has He taught you, lately? You don't have to go to Sunday School to be schooled by the Holy Spirit. As a Christian, He resides inside of you as your fulness of God. He leads, directs and guides into all truth. Well, He's been speaking to me lately and this is the result. I've got it burning in my bones! What are we going to do? The world out there needs us!

I've heard it said that there is an emptiness that is God-shaped inside each of us and people fill it with everything but the Lord, until they have reached the end of themselves. The last resort is the Church or the one who goes there to inquire about this one called—Jesus. You can tell them that He is the only One who can fix it. We can meet the lack and we certainly don't need to give them any flack!

What every one needs is the saving knowledge of Christ, the Son of God. To receive the Born-again experience, a re-birthing that will change them forever that wherever they go, they walk and talk this message of salvation by Jesus Christ. They are remade by the reality of God—like LOVE.

Maybe, if we did more talking of Jesus outside the church, there would be more working inside the Church. I'm just thinking out loud. The Church is our base out of which we work to lead others to Jesus.

Maybe, just maybe, the world needs to see the Church at work outside the church, if you know what I mean. I've had my wrist swatted by the Lord for not showing forth His honor and glory and praise in public. I have cried out to the Master, *"Okay Lord, you have to do something about my temper."* He did, He took it before I could do a thing about it when I needed it taken care of. One time in a business I owned years ago, a woman slapped me and I had never been slapped before. Collene's temper rose up within her (that's me, of course). When I stood up, the Lord intervened and I didn't do anything in response. I merely turned the other cheek. She picked up my glasses, handed them to me and apologized.

I closed my shop and went to church. That lady became a Christian after that incident because she saw Christ likeness in action. That day taught me a lot.

The Church is—a SAVING PLACE. Our Savior died to save our souls and build His House. It is the House of God that travelled with Abraham throughout the desert and their wanderings and is just as important today. The place to be saved and to learn God's will and purpose for you is in the House of God. If you are not going, find one who is teaching and preaching the Word, that will pray with you when you need it.

45

The Valley of Decision

This life holds many decisions that we make through the years. We decide to get up every morning if we can. We decide to marry or stay single, live for the Lord or not, to be happy or to be sad, to mess our lives up or make something of ourselves.

How many years since you have seen someone on their face before the Lord? How long since you have seen a person who has recently accepted the Lord and you can see a smile where there was none. Both of these are results of choices.

In the Garden of Eden, they could choose anything they wanted except to eat of the tree of knowledge. That set into motion a plan that has been like the reflection of God's character to us. He made us in His image and in that action He gave us the ability to choose. We can choose to live for Him or not. If we believe that He is, we know Him as a loving God; Who fights our battles.

I personally have made some very dumb moves in my life and have found the Lord to be as tough as He needs to be or as gentle in chastening. There have been times, He has let me try it on my own. He knows how stubborn I can be.

In the past few days, I spoke to a young man at the VA Office in Nashville, Tennessee. He reminded me so much of some of the young people I have known in the past. He had a sweet spirit and it seemed as if there was no rebellion in him.

We went in the doctor's office and he was still there when I came out with my husband. I spoke to him, but when I walked out the door I had to go back and talk to him some more. God was dealing with my heart heavily and I asked him if he went to church and he said yes. I began to tell him that God had called him to a ministry and he said cutely, *"Stop it."* I said I could not stop. I knew that others had told him the same thing. Now I had never seen this young man before, but I knew in my heart of hearts he had a calling on his life. I felt his fear, but told him I would be praying and don't run from what God had for him.

It was as if he was a child of mine. Of course, he reminded me of others I had talked to and prayed for through the years.

We walk through a *valley of decision.* My boldness may have frightened him, but how much time do we have left in this world. We have to be bold and do what God wants us to do. God loved us so much that He sent His Son to die for us, what more can we do to repay that debt of love.

We must trust Him and when He tells us to do something, we have to do it. He doesn't tell us to hurt people, or to be mean. He sends us to be His hands and feet and minister the Gospel to others.

Many of us want to tell the older ones in the Church to stop it when God is speaking to them through those old ladies who pray and walk in the Spirit of God or those older gentlemen who know what God is telling them.

47

We Can't Do Just Anything We Want To!

If I can be faulted for anything, it is plain speech. Just look at that title. I am not a politician. I am not running for office. I am not politically correct. And, at my age, I don't feel like holding back any words. I am motivated by the idea that generally our population feels they can do whatever they want and get away with it. That is far from the truth.

If you remember, in *the Book of Acts*, there was a couple named *Ananias and Sapphira* and they had made a promise to the Lord. The punishment was severe, but no man had to carry it out. (Recall, in the early church, they adhered to communal living and surrendered everything to a common fund for redistribution) In *Acts 5:1, "But a certain man named Ananaias, with Sapphira his wife, sold a possession, and kept back part of the price, his wife also being privy to it, and brought a certain, and laid it at the apostles' feet. But Peter said, Ananias, why hath Satan filled thine heart to lie to the Holy Ghost, and to keep back part of the price of the land? Whilest it remained, was it not thine own? And after it was sold, was it not in thine own power? Why hast thou conceived this thing in thine heart? Thou hast not lied unto men, but unto God. And Ananaias hearing these words fell down, and gave up the ghost: and great fear came on all them that heard these things. And the young men arose, bound him up, and carried him out, and buried him."* The Scripture goes on to say that within about three hours time, his wife did the same thing without knowing what had happened to her husband. She also chose to lie to Peter and was struck and taken out to be buried by her husband.

THERE IS NO EVIL THING DONE IN THIS WORLD IN THIS LIFE THAT WILL NOT BE VINDICATED. God sees what we think, what we have planned and He is the compensator of the just and a condemner of the unjust. He will see to it that the appropriate judgment is passed. He is the only One to rightly judge the whole universe.

Maybe we consider cheating on our taxes. It may not be seen by man, but God knows the thoughts and intents of our hearts. How about an unhealthy view of children? How about a view of another you see at church every Sunday that would appear unseemly if known by others? What about robbing God by not paying a full tithe in the offering plate and still giving the appearance to the treasurer that it is a true ten percent?

What about singing in church *"God loves the children of the world . . . Red and Yellow, Black and White"* and you harbor ill will against someone at work because of their color? Is that enough? Do you get the idea? Our God has the ability to know every thought and every deed of all of us, His creation. There is more to life than meets our eyes.

179

Our lives are an open book to the Almighty!

People don't like to be corrected, but they want to do anything they choose to do. With God, punishment delayed is not punishment denied. There will be a payday, someday. Some of the kids who would come into Walmart would come in crying because they didn't want to get into the shopping carts. They wanted to touch the toys or the groceries or pick up the candy. They didn't want to be deprived of putting their hands on anything and everything they could touch in the store. Even though we are the children of God, let's not act like "children."

Several years before I retired, a small boy slapped the woman he was with and looked at me with his three or four year old grin and said, *"I slapped her."* I said, *"I saw that and you shouldn't do that."* He just laughed.

You can forget about laughing at God. Some of the things we say are a slap in the face of God. Some of the things we do are a stench in the nostrils of God. It came back to Ananias and Sapphira in a serious judgment that showed God's dislike for lying.

Bernie made off with a lot of folks' money. He has not shown any sorrow for stealing not thousands, not millions, but billions from people. He was not sorrowful for the suffering his family went through when this all came to light. His son committed suicide over his daddy's dastardly deeds. No remorse, but God will recompense in the other real world. Don't worry... it will be sifted out in the end, like everything else in this world, no matter how small. Even the amount of only a d-o-l-l-a-r . . . . .

"Be not deceived, God is not mocked. That what you sow you will surely reap." There is PAYBACK or BACK PAY. You might not see it now, but it is coming.

When I talk about the other real world, people don't believe in the spirit realm, but there is a Heaven and a Hell. What will our back pay be?

Christ covers us with His blood and that is the only thing that will save us from Hell. Christ is the door to Heaven, without Him, there is no Heaven for us.

48

Your Thoughts Can Drag You Down

Day in and day out (that is our dream sequences), we linger and malinger in the vast domain of thought. We stop and spend time on a bad memory or we cannot get past a hurtful incident that provokes us to anger. We want to cry or be caught up in the fantasy of *"Days of Our Lives."*

I know I'm talking to my gender but you men, please, stay with me. It's for you, too.

I had some surgery a long time ago that was relatively minor but, with my recovery, I got involved in the dailies of the "soap operas." There was an insurance agent who came to the house each month and picked up his payment for a policy that we carried, years ago. One month when I was so caught up in my daily stories of soaps, another agent showed up. Remember, I had surgery and was trying to escape my personal, painful reality. I inquired about the other agent and was devastated to find out that the young man had committed suicide. That brought me to my senses. It hit me hard that I had been so involved in my day to day serials that I had passed by an opportunity to minister to someone who was on the verge of suicide. I stopped that daily vigil of soaps and got into the Word and asked God to forgive me. I had let my guard down and had been wallowing in my own little world after surgery. My mind was let to wander through a story line that I had control over. Mind you, I might not have had any effect on the young man's outcome, nonetheless, just a word could have influenced him to know that someone cared about him and that the Lord was the sustainer through any stressful situation. After that, they couldn't advertise enough soap on those soaps to clean up my mind. I had to do it with the *"washing of water by the Word."*

When we get lost in all that negative stuff that we have

voluntarily wrapped ourselves in, I am reminded of *1 Peter 5:7* that says this: *"Be sober, be vigilant: because your adversary the devil, as a roaring lion, walketh about, seeking whom he may devour."* Sometimes the main battlefield is in the mind. I believe our adversary roars through our minds, just like he does everywhere else. If that is so, the enemy is walking around in the recesses of our minds and his sole intent is to devour us. If we dwell on the bad, the devil has a tool to use against us. Old Satan can amplify the trifling of our thoughts and build them up to the point that they are blown entirely out of proportion to reality. Each of us has sundry memories, all those bad conglomerations, that should be applied to our aptitude to assist others to progress farther, faster to a more virtuous life, beyond what we have attained thus far, ourselves.

I know I can't help everyone. Believe me, my son used to remind me that I couldn't fix everyone, but just a word, a gesture of kindness, or acknowledgment of someone might calm an inner storm or breed some confidence in a sagging spirit.

A few months ago, my husband whom many of you know as "Krazy Kent" was in a funk over his tour of duty to Vietnam because he had to send in a report to the VA as to his combat experiences. It was a fresh reminder of bad wartime encounters. He was talking to a mental health professional at the VA center in Murfreesboro last week and remembered what got him out of his personality "flat lining."

We were at our favorite eating place, Ryan's in Crossville with a waitress who knew us well and overheard us talking about how he needed to come out of this low point. She simply interrupted us and said, *"You need to do right; you need to think right!"* Those few words pulled him out immediately. And, that's how we described it to the professional. It didn't take a professional to do the job. It was a few sincere words from a waitress. And, the last week, we reminded her of how helpful she was back then and that helped her back for the day. That's the circular motion of good going around and around!

II Timothy 1:7 says, *"For God hath not given us a spirit of fear [fearfulness]; but of power, and of love, and of a sound mind."* I want to keep my mind in check so my life will be reigned in to do the will of God. God's will is that no man or woman should perish and that all should have life to the extent of wholesome abundance. When you wake up in the morning, it should not be, *"Good lord, morning"* but *"Good morning, Lord and good morning world!"*

The Lord has thoughts for us for good in *Jeremiah 11:29*. We give less thought to this: God is as concerned about us mentally as He is spiritually and emotionally and physically. Jesus wants all of us, our thoughts, too! He is an upper, not a downer!

Conclusion

Many have not accepted Christ, but He is the only way to Heaven. There may be those of you who disagree, however, to me with the way He has proven Himself to me through storms and every manner of tribulation in my personal life—I know He is the way.

Revelations 13 tells us that Satan will be defeated *by the blood of the Lamb and our Testimony.* That Lamb is Jesus Christ, created from the foundation of the world.

I've been through rape, divorce, both parents gone before I was thirty, both brothers gone in the last two years, but the Lord has never cast me aside or turned away from me. He has ministered to me through each situation that has come across the path of my life—I trust Him no matter what comes.

My husband is a victim of Agent Orange and God has equipped me with the faith to pray for his healing and for his comfort through the treatments. When he relives the horror of someone coming after him or things he can't remember, I reach over and pray and God puts him back to sleep. When a nurse practitioner told Kent that he had six months to live, two years ago; I told him that we were not going to pine or grieve, but we were going to trust the Lord.

Jesus gave me the faith to move away from my lifetime home of Texas to Tennessee. Kent wanted to retire in his home region and here we are and because I trusted the Lord, we have been blessed exceeding abundantly above anything we could think or ask.

If you have not accepted Jesus, you are missing out on your one way ticket to Heaven and I don't want any of you left behind. I want hugs from all of you. I accepted Jesus at eight years old and here I am at the age of 72, believing as much or even many times more than I did in my youth because He has shown me He is true.

If you have not accepted Jesus, please pray this prayer with me:

"Lord Jesus, I ask You to come into my heart and forgive me of all my sin. I turn away from all my sin and thank you for forgiving me of all my sin and thank you for saving my soul. I ask you to fill me up with your Holy Spirit that there will no room for anything but your presence in me, I ask this in the Name of Jesus Christ."

If you just prayed this, I am praying for you now. *"Lord thank You for my new brother or sister and I ask that You teach them by Your precious Holy Spirit. Your Word says that You will lead us into all truth and Lord thank You for increasing our family in the Name of Jesus Christ."*

Now because You prayed that prayer, You have opened the door to Your heart as Jesus said on *Revelation 3:20, "Behold I stand at the door and knock: and if any man hear my voice, and will open the door, I will come in to him, and sup with him and he with me."*

When you pray, pray in the Name of Jesus Christ and God hears and answers your prayers. Knowing Christ as your Savior gives you priority to get your prayers through. *John 14:13-14, "And whatsoever you ask in my name (Jesus Christ) that will I do, that the Father may be glorified in the Son. If ye shall ask anything in my name, I will do it."*

This is how we **"Poke holes in the darkness** for others." You are now a child of God for asking Jesus to come into your heart and saving your soul. This makes you a child of the King.

Let's **poke holes in the darkness** for others together now. God bless you and keep you. He is coming soon. Now you are ready if you asked Jesus into your heart. I look forward to my heavenly hugs.

Start your day off right with God's Word.

Add to your morning routine this wonderful
refreshing collection of writings by many
well known Ministers and emerging Christian Authors.

Over 125 writings by 60 different authors, encouraging, faith-filled, inspirational and all about our AWESOME GOD.